GOD'S ANSWER TO MAN'S SIN

By
HYMAN J. APPELMAN
Author, "Ye Must Be Born Again"

Third Edition

ZONDERVAN PUBLISHING HOUSE
Grand Rapids, Michigan

EIGHT FORTY-SEVEN OTTAWA AVENUE
GRAND RAPIDS, MICHIGAN

PREFACE

ALTHOUGH these sermons are published by request, there is but one reason for sending them out into the world. The Lord has used them in the salvation of tens of thousands of souls, Jews and Gentiles, young and old. They are put out with the passionate prayer that the reading of them may win others to Christ.

Every one of them was preached and written in the pressure, the drive, the heat of evangelistic service. There was little time for grammar, rhetoric, oratory, polish. Do not judge them too harshly. They come, each of them, from the burning soul, from the burdened heart, from the longing mind, from the weeping eyes of this poor Jew. Read them! Pass them on to others! Pray for their preacher.

God be with you. God bless you. God use you in the winning of precious souls to a saving acceptance of the Son of God. In Jesus' name. Amen.

HYMAN APPELMAN

Fort Worth, Texas

CONTENTS

I

GOD'S ANSWER TO MAN'S SIN

For the wages of sin is death; but the gift of God is eternal life through Jesus Christ our Lord.
—Rom. 6:23

IN ONE tremendous sentence, Paul the Apostle sums up the Bible, the need of man, the provision of God. In one smashing declaration, Paul gathers up all we need to know of the plan of redemption. There are many who say they should like to become Christians but they do not know enough of the Book. They want time to study the Word of God. Most of them never get to it. It is just one more trap of the devil. In this brilliantly, lucidly simple word, Paul strips every sinner of this alibi. Romans 6:23 contains enough to save every believing and to damn every unbelieving soul on earth. Clearly, definitely, simply, unmistakably, the verse is divided into three thoughts: first, Sin is Death; second, Salvation is through Christ; third, This salvation is the free gift of God.

1. *Sin is Death.* The ages have proved the truth of Paul's contention that the consequences of sin is death. It was death when Adam and Eve were driven from Eden and the mark of mortality was placed on their foreheads. It was death when the flood waters of God's

wrath deluged the earth, destroying every living, breathing thing outside of the ark. Every floating corpse of man and beast rocking on the terrible waves was an amen to Paul's assertion. It was death when fire fell from heaven, utterly obliterating Sodom and Gomorrah. Every smouldering pile, every charred heap was a "Yea, verily" to our text. It was death when the death angel stalked through the Land of Egypt on that evil night, claiming the firstborn in every Gentile home in that fearful visitation of God's wrath. Every moaning, groaning shriek that rose from the overburdened hearts of fathers and mothers that God-cursed night was a positive demonstration of the eternal truth of this contention. It was death when the coming together of the Red Sea waters swallowed the chivalry of Egypt. It was death when the heavy-handed angel of God slew Sennacherib's 185,000 Assyrian warriors beleaguering Jerusalem. It was death when Christ Jesus bled out His life on Calvary's cross. It was death when Titus inundated Jerusalem with the blood bath of thousands of slain Jews. It was death when the maddened Serbian student shot the Austrian arch-duke and deluged the world in the blood of the last great war. Every floating flood corpse, every smouldering heap of Sodom's cataclysm, every dead Egyptian firstborn, every water-logged Egyptian warrior, every plague-stricken Assyrian warrior, every drop of Christ's blood, every cross-marked grave in Flander's field, every tomb of every unknown soldier that graces the capital of every civilized nation, is a shouting, eternal amen to Paul's dictum, "The wages of sin is death." It was death! It is death! It shall continue to be death until Christ, the Conqueror, vanishes that last dread enemy.

The wages of sin is death today here in our midst.

It is physical death, mental death, moral death, spiritual death, the second death. It is death to character, to personality, to ambition, to reputation, to love, to influence, to life, to homes, to businesses, to schools, to churches.

It is universal death. The Jew, the Gentile, the man, the woman, the child, "the soul that sinneth, it shall die." There is no escape from it. There is no alibying it. There is no denying it, no defying it, no hiding from it. We carry its germs in our own bodies. We breathe them in with the air. We draw them in with the water and food. The whole universe is under the curse, the condemnation, the consequences of sin, which is death. The rich man has not enough riches to overcome it. The poor man is not lowly enough to obviate it. The king in his throne room, the queen in her boudoir, the philosopher in his classic study, the harlot in her den, the peasant turning the clods; they all look alike and they are all alike to the Grim Reaper. Not all the schemes, not all the programs, not all the organizations, not all the proposals of man have in any way ameliorated this fearful fact.

It is inescapable death. You will find it wherever men gather. Civilization is no barrier to it, and crudeness cannot stop it. Brilliancy is no obstacle, and barbarism cannot stem it. You will find funeral trains in the heathen heart of Africa as in the loftier life of America. There is no excuse; there is no escape; there is no exception. It cannot be bought off, reasoned off, pushed off. Its bony terror is as inescapable as the thoughts of our minds or the beats of our hearts. Surely, if men realized it, if women saw it, there would be an end to the mad chase after the physical and the temporal and a hastening to the pursuance of the eternal. Our whole

system — social, political, economic, even religious,
would be changed over night if by some act of God's
grace the inevitability of death were pressed upon the
souls of mankind.

Not only is it universal death, not only is it inescapable death, but by the authority of God's Word, sin
is eternal death, the second death, the bottomless pit
of a burning, everlasting hell. That, too, is the true
consequence of sin. Solve the problem of sin, smash
the hold of Satan, stop the inroads of temptation, and
hell has lost its terrors, while death has been banished
from the scheme of eternity. There is an eternal,
burning, tormenting hell, a banishment from the presence of God, a place of ceaseless, hopeless, helpless
remorse waiting for all those who die with their sins
unconfessed and unforgiven. That is the decree of God.
That is the dictum of eternity. That is the declaration
of the ages.

But there is a way of escape from the curse, from
the condemnation, from the doom, from the damnation
of sin. It is a God-promised, a Jesus-provided, a Holy-
Spirit-proffered way. It is the Bible way, the gospel
way, the way of the cross, the way of the blood, the
way of Calvary. It cost God all that He was and all that
He had, but He offers it freely to the children of men.
That is my second word.

2. *Salvation is through Jesus Christ.* In Christ
Jesus there is absolute, total, eternal, effective salvation
for every soul to the ends of the earth. You say,
"Preacher, how can you say that? You don't know all
the people in the world. Why, you do not even know
all of us here to whom you are preaching. How can
you be so dogmatically certain that there is salvation
for all of us?" Beloved, I may not know you. I may

not know all the people in the world. But I know the
Bible. I know the Lord. It is because I know the Book
and the Book's God that I can so unhesitatingly offer
salvation to every one of you on the terms of the gospel.
The Bible gives us three foundations, three certainties
concerning that redemption. They are all based on the
person and work of the Lord Jesus Christ.

First, Jesus came to save. He Himself said, "The Son
of man is come not to be ministered unto, but to minister
and to give his life a ransom for many." "The Son of
man is come to seek and to save that which was lost."
God said about Him, "Thou shalt call his name Jesus,
because he shall save his people from their sins." That
was His mission. That was His ministry. For that He
left His home in heaven. For that He took upon Himself the circumscribed life of a man. For that He
humbled Himself in the carpenter's shop of Nazareth.
For that He limited Himself to the fare of the poor,
denying Himself even the bare comforts of a home and
an affectionate family. For that He preached the Word,
healed the sick, cleansed the lepers, raised the dead.
For that He prayed through the lonely nights with the
weight of the world's woes upon Him. For that He
wept over Jerusalem. For that He sweated blood in
dark Gethsemane. For that He died on the cross. Yes,
there is salvation for every one of you because Jesus
Christ came to save.

He died to save. In His own precious body, on
Calvary's bitter tree, He bore the sins of every soul
among us. "He was made to be sin for us, who knew
no sin, that we might be made the righteousness of
God in him." "Christ hath redeemed us from the curse
of the Law, being made a curse for us, for it is written,
Cursed is everyone which hangeth on a tree." "For-

asmuch as you know that you were not redeemed with
corruptible things, as silver and gold; . . . but with
the precious blood of Christ, as a lamb without blemish
and without spot." "All we like sheep have gone astray;
we have turned everyone to his own way; but the Lord
hath laid on him the iniquity of us all." These Scripture
passages are clearly definite in their declaration that
Christ, the Son of God, died for our sins, died to save us.
That death is the seal of the covenant between the Father
and the Son by virtue of which covenant we are redeemed when we come to God through faith in Christ.
The blood of Jesus poured out on Calvary's cross ties
the hands of God in two ways. He cannot save any
sinner outside of the blood; He must save every sinner
who comes claiming that atonement. You may be as
certain of the forgiveness of your sins as you are of
the fact that Jesus died under their burden on Calvary's
cross.

Jesus lives to save. Were the cross the end of the
life of the Master, were Joseph's tomb still sealed with
the grip of death and the grave, our salvation would
be a matter of deep doubt, of bitter misgivings. We
could not be sure of the immaculate conception of
Jesus, of His sinless life, of His matchless teachings,
of His mighty works, of His healing, saving, keeping
power. The foundations of our faith are laid in the
verity of the resurrection and the eternal, heavenly life
of the Redeemer. But we have the Word of God and
the testimony of nineteen hundred years of Christian
history that the crucified Son of God did rise from the
dead, that He did go back to His Father in glory, that
in and through the Holy Spirit He has been changing
the destinies of men, of nations, of the world. By faith
we, each of us, may experience a personal, definite,

dependable indwelling of the living Christ. It is not something to explain, something to reason or argue about. It is a heart-filling possession to be obtained by a glad surrender to the Lord. By that experiential knowledge we come to the conclusion that Jesus lives to save. He walks with us, talks with us, guides us, sustains us, empowers us, enlightens us, ennobles us, enables us, in short, saves us from the drag, the drain, the drought of the slavery of this world into the joy and the fulness of fellowship with and service in God. It is what the sacred writer sings of when he writes, "Wherefore he is able also to save them to the utter-most that come unto God by him, seeing he ever liveth to make intercession for them." Yes, there is salvation for you because Jesus lives to save.

3. Now, my last word: *This Salvation is the Free Gift of God's Love.* "For by grace are ye saved, through faith; and that not of yourselves, it is the gift of God: not of works, lest any man should boast." "For we ourselves also were sometimes foolish, disobedient, deceived, serving divers lusts and pleasures, living in malice and envy, hateful and hating one another. But after that the kindness and love of God, our Savior, towards man appeared, not by works of righteousness which we have done, but according to his mercy he saved us, by the washing of regeneration, and renewing of the Holy Ghost; which he shed on us abundantly through Jesus Christ our Savior; that being justified by his grace, we should be made heirs according to the hope of eternal life."

It is free because it is priceless, beyond human value and computation. There is nothing man knows with which this salvation may be compared. Take all of the blessings God has showered down upon us, add to them all of the manifold material treasures, properties, possessions, accomplishments, achievements, precious things in all the earth, pile them into one glittering heap until they outshine the noonday sun in its splendor. Place by the side of the grand mountain one precious drop of the blood of Jesus. The treasured pile will cheapen by comparison into shoddy, into fool's gold. Compare the possession of salvation, of immortal life and bliss, with any earthly belongings, and you will understand what I mean by the pricelessness of this mightiest of all of God's benefits.

It is free because it has been paid for. It was paid for in the humbling of the Son of God, when He stripped Himself of His heavenly glory to come down upon the earth to live the life of a circumscribed Galilean peasant Jew. It was paid for in the blood sweat of Gethsemane. It was paid for in the scourging of the Roman injustice. It was paid for in the loneliness, in the shame, in the heartache, in the heartbreak, in the blood-letting, in the blood-shedding of Calvary's cross. God cannot, God has not, God will not, God does not require any price from us poor sinners save the coin of repentance and faith.

It is free because it is offered freely to whomsoever will come and take it. The Bible is very definite on that point. In many places, in many ways, in precept and in parable, the Holy-Spirit-indited Scriptures offer the blood of Christ, the bread and the water of life, very freely to all comers. For nineteen hundred years this free salvation has been proffered to the children of men. Multiplied myriads of every clime, country, condition, race, have found their way to the Fountain, even blood-stained Calvary, and have drunk deeply and freely of the flowing blood and water to their own pardon and eternal joy.

The Holy Spirit invites you to that salvation. Every saving promise, every urgent appeal, every wonderful, tenderly wooing word that He can invent He urges upon you to come and be saved, to come fleeing from the wrath to come, to come to escape from the wages of sin. You are standing at the cross-roads. On the one hand, the Lord is tugging at your heart, pulling at your soul, offering you the blood of Christ for the remission of your sins. On the other hand, Satan is striving with all his hellish power to keep you from accepting the gospel invitation. The decision is yours. It is either the wages of sin or the gift of God. It is either Christ or Satan, God or sin, salvation or damnation, life or death, heaven or hell. Your decision will make the difference. The devil will not let you go without a struggle. You must tear loose from him by an act of will. You must step over the line to the Savior. God, for Christ's sake, will do the rest.

Some years ago, the superb young English evangelist, Henry Moorehouse, was invited to a Welsh mining town to hold a revival. The few Christian people there built for him a humble tabernacle—earth floor, four walls, a roof. He started preaching twice each day. The crowds came. Souls were converted. A church was organized. The meeting began to stir the town, becoming the talk of the streets. One night as Moorehouse started for the pulpit, two of the church-members, men, called him to one side.

"Brother Henry," they said, "some of us believe you had better close the meeting tonight and leave town."

"Why, brethren," questioned the preacher, "what is the matter? What have I done?"

"It is nothing that you have done, Brother Henry; it is what is going to be done to you."

"What's going to be done to me, and who is going to do it? You may as well tell me. I am not afraid. Besides, I cannot make up my mind properly until I know all the facts."

"Brother Moorehouse," said one of the men, "there is a wicked fellow in this town by the name of Ike Miller. He is the vilest, lowest, lewdest white man we know anything about. He hates preachers, despises the church, abuses Christians, curses the Lord and the Bible. He told some of us to tell you that unless you close the meeting tonight he's coming tomorrow night to break it up and pistol whip you out of town."

Henry bowed his head in silent thought. "Brethren," he said, "I feel very definitely that the Lord has brought me to preach to you. He will take care of me and of this meeting. I am not running. What does this Ike look like?"

They told him. All the next day the preacher scouted and hunted all over the town to find Ike, to talk to him, but he could not locate him. That night the tabernacle was packed and jammed. Henry gave out a hymn, then another. He called on someone to pray. The crowd sang again. The evangelist read his Scripture, announced his subject, led the congregation in another season of prayer, then began to preach. He had just well started when the door opened with a bang to admit the bulky, burly form of Ike Miller. Moorehouse recognized him from the description he had received. Ike walked all the way to the front, sat down on the very first bench, and looked up at the preacher, as if to say, "Well, go ahead and do your stuff," and settled down.

Henry closed his Bible. Once more he lifted his face to God to breathe a silent prayer. Then slowly, gently, clearly, he announced a new text, "For God so loved the world that he gave his only begotten Son that whosoever believeth in him should not perish but have everlasting life." He preached a sermon on the love of God that would have melted the heart of a statue. Finishing, he called the people to their feet and led out in the invitation hymn. No one moved. Some few sang. In the middle of the second verse, Ike Miller turned about and heavily stomped out of the room. The crowd broke up at once. The men crowded around the preacher.

"Henry, of all the idiotic things that any preacher ever did, you've done the worst tonight. What does a man like Ike Miller know about the love of God? Why did you not tell him about the wrath of God and the doom of sin?"

Moorehouse bowed his head as the hot tears scalded down his cheeks. "Brethren," he plead, "pray for me. Perhaps I have made a mistake, but I was trying to follow the leadership of the Holy Spirit."

But the Holy Spirit had known what He was about. It was He who had spoken through the preacher to the sin-cursed heart of the wicked miner. Ike Miller left the tabernacle blindly and staggered down the main street of the town. He passed saloons, gambling joints, places of infinitely worse repute. Men and women tried to stop him, but he shook them off and kept on walking. He came to the end of the street, turned to the right, walked about a half mile out on a narrow country road, came to a tumbled-down gate in a dilapidated fence enclosing a one-room, weatherboard shack, so old and decrepit that the light could be seen through the spaces between the boards. He made good money but drank and gambled and caroused it away.

He plodded toward the door and pushed it open. The room was bare. There was an old stove in one corner, a bed, a pallet, a table, and two rickety chairs. His wife was seated at the table working on some darning in a sewing-basket. His two children, a girl about ten and a boy about seven, were on each side of their mother, fussing over something in her lap. They heard the door and looked up to see their father come in. Their little faces blanched with fear. The mother stood up, motioned the children behind her, and slowly backed up toward the bed. The boy and girl swiftly crawled under the bed. They thought the father was drunk, coming to beat up on them. The mother was willingly anxious to take all the abuse upon herself to spare the children. Ike knew what they were doing. He was a rotten sinner, but he had plenty of sense. His heart strained in his great body; his eyes began to smart with unshed tears. Walking into the room, he stretched out his arms and gathered his wife into them. "Lassie," he said, "you need not fear anymore. God has brought you a new husband tonight." He pressed her to his heart while she sobbed. After a bit he released her. Kneeling by the side of the bed, he wheedled his children out. They crept up, saw their mother's tears, and began to cry also.

Ike embraced them, petted them, comforted them, kissed them, cried with them. After a while, he turned to his wife. "Lass, we ought to pray." All four knelt at the old table. The woman began to pray but broke down. All the pain, the torment, the passion of the abused years came out in her loud weeping. The children sobbed with her.

Ike raised his voice. "Lord," he said, and stopped.
"Master," and stopped. "Savior," and stopped.
"Father," and stopped. He did so want to pray, but
he did not know how. His sinful heart broke. The long
restrained flood of tears swept him in a mighty emotion
of penitence and longing. Somehow there came to his
mind an old prayer verse he'd learned at the knees of
his mother. Lifting his head, he wept out:

> *"Gentle Jesus, meek and mild,*
> *Look upon a little child,*
> *Pity my simplicity,*
> *Suffer me to come to Thee."*

Beloved, Jesus reached down from heaven and with
His own heart's blood washed away that man's sins.
He made him a child of God, called him to preach the
Word, used him to win thousands for Christ.

God, for Christ's sake, will do as much for you if
you will come, accepting the free gift of His love, even
eternal life through Jesus Christ.

"I AM DEBTOR"

I am debtor both to the Greeks, and to the Barbarians; both to the wise and to the unwise. So, as much as in me is, I am ready to preach the gospel to you that are at Rome also. For I am not ashamed of the gospel of Christ: for it is the power of God unto salvation to every one that believeth; to the Jew first, and also to the Greek.—ROM. 1: 14-16

THIS is the heart of Paul's theology, the very soul of Paul's religion, the essence of his consecrated devotion. In three terrific statements, Paul lifts us to the heights of Christian faith and devotion. Understand them and you will have apprehended the motives of the life of this matchless servant of Christ.

Surely this man, Paul, is worth studying, worth knowing, worth following. Without any further introduction, therefore, let us consider the mighty message out of the burning heart of this magnificent minister of Christ. To help you understand and to help me preach, may we think together of these three statements of Paul:

   I. I AM NOT ASHAMED

   II. I AM DEBTOR

   III. I AM READY

I. *I Am Not Ashamed*

"I am not ashamed of the gospel" is a description of Paul's attitude toward the Word of God that he had been commissioned to proclaim to a lost world. The gospel had an entirely different standing in those days from that which it occupies today. The cross was a mark of shame, of obloquy, of criminality. To most men Jesus was a mad man at best, a malefactor at worst. His message was a mockery, a mediocre statement of ethics that could in no way compare with the philosophy of Aristotle and Socrates. The whole world was against Him, yet Paul could stand facing this same world and cry, *"I am not ashamed of the gospel."* Yea, neither are we!

With Paul, we are not ashamed of its compiler— God. It is not the work of man, of groups of men, of schools of men. It is the inerrant, unchangeable, unmistakable, eternal, universal Word of God dictated by the Holy Spirit for the guidance of the ages. It is without fault, without flaw, without fear, without favor. It speaks to the heart of the man, the woman, the child, of every clime, of every country, of every continent, of every condition. It is positive, permanent, powerful. It was as true nineteen hundred years ago as it is today, as it will be when Christ comes again. It is as necessary this hour as it has been through the generations that have passed, and it will be for as long as the world stands.

Together with Paul, we are not ashamed of its contents—salvation. It alone is the bread of life and directs to the fountain of the water of life. It alone promises, provides, and proffers eternal life. The Lamb of God, which taketh away the sin of the world, is its theme. It alone describes the way of the cross that leads home. It alone sustains the pilgrim over the steep ascent that leads to God and to glory. It alone teaches and offers the redemption of souls, the remission of sins, the reconciliation of sinners. The world is consciously and unconsciously hungry for its eternal deliverance.

Together with Paul, we are not ashamed of its consequences—the power of God unto salvation to every one who believeth. Twelve men, poor, humble, lowly, mediocre, with no organization, with no finances, with no standing, started out to preach. That trickle became a brook; that brook became a river; that river became an ocean of saved souls seeking sinners for a sacrificial, sovereign Savior. Their message has changed individuals, cities, nations, continents, a whole world. It has "rescued the perishing, cared for the dying, snatched them in pity from sin and the grave, wept o'er the erring one, lifted the fallen, told them of Jesus, the mighty to save." It has built churches, established schools, organized hospitals, orphanages, old folks' homes. It has emancipated women, ennobled and educated children, and alleviated old age. Wherever its cross has been lifted, its message proclaimed, barbarism has been changed to civilization and culture, and the brutality of man to man has been ameliorated by the sacrificial constraint of the lowly, loving Nazarene. Most of all, best of all, loftiest of all, it has redeemed and released souls from the slavery of sin, from the storminess of self. It has made saints out of sinners and angels out of demons.

I know a man now in glory, a reprobate, a thief, a forger, an outcast, an outlaw. Christ found him, saved him, sanctified him, stirred him. I stood by his side in a gospel mission in a western city and, having finished my sermon, heard him in a passionate, tear-strained plea, appeal to sinners to come to Christ. His name is Jimmy Goodheart; the place, the Sunshine Mission; the city, Denver, Colorado. That's what the gospel did.

I know another man intimately. He was alien-born, a lawyer, crooked, careless, indifferent to the claims of society, with the passion for money-making running riot in his veins, as far from religion and God as a man can be. Christ sought him, saved him, sent him. He is before you now, preaching Christ to you. That is what the gospel has done.

II. *I Am Debtor*

Paul goes on with the burning enthusiasm of his soul for the message of salvation. With every nerve in his body astretch with gratitude to the Savior of his soul, with tear-dimmed eyes, looking out upon a lost, dying, judgment-bound world, he cries, *"I am debtor."*

That was a declaration. It drummed in his heart! It throbbed in his mind! It burned in his soul! It was his meat by day and his travail by night! By that he lived! By that he was sustained! For that he preached! For that he toiled! For that he suffered! For that, when in God's wisdom, the time came, he died! He was debtor! So are we!

Together with Paul, we are debtors to Christ. We are debtors to Him for creation. It was He who fashioned our members in the wombs of our mothers. It was He who called us into being. It was He who gave us our sound minds and our sound bodies. We are debtors to Him for preservation, for every bite of food, for every drop of water, for every breath of air that has entered into our bodies from the first breath that we drew to this good hour. Think, beloved, of all the

mighty, munificent, magnificent blessings Christ has
showered down upon us throughout the days of our lives.
It will take this day and tomorrow and the next, beloved, the lifetime of every one of us, to tell the sum
of all the benedictions that have been poured out upon
us in all the days of our being.

But most of all, above all, beyond all, are we debtors
for our redemption. In agony, in loneliness, in shame,
in travail, in blood, in death on the cruel cross of
Calvary, Christ provided our salvation. He built a
bridge across hell, paved a way into heaven, provided
a mansion in glory. Surely our blood must run faster,
our hearts beat harder, our eyes fill with tears of gratitude at the measure of His love and sacrifice for us.
Surely we can cry with the poet:

> *When I survey the wondrous cross*
> *On which the Prince of Glory died,*
> *My richest gain I count but loss,*
> *And pour contempt on all my pride.*
>
> *Forbid it, Lord, that I should boast,*
> *Save in the death of Christ, my God;*
> *All the vain things that charm me most,*
> *I sacrifice them to His blood.*
>
> *See, from His head, His hands, His feet,*
> *Sorrow and love flow mingled down;*
> *Did e'er such love and sorrow meet,*
> *Or thorns compose so rich a crown?*
>
> *Were the whole realm of nature mine,*
> *That were a present far too small;*
> *Love so amazing, so divine,*
> *Demands my soul, my life, my all.*

But that is not all. Together with Paul, we are
debtors to the conquerors of the past. Think of the
mighty-hearted martyrs, men, women, children, that

cemented together with their hearts' blood the walls of Zion, the church that you and I so thoroughly enjoy today.

We are debtors to Peter for dying crucified, head down, in the Roman arena. We are debtors to Paul for his emaciated, striped back, his bleeding body, for his days of imprisonment in the dark, dank, dismal Asiatic and European jails, for the blood that he spilt when he was beheaded for a testimony. There are others, many others. Time is too short for me to enumerate them.

Think of the arenas of the Roman world, saturated, inundated, baptized, with the heroic blood of the early Christians, who went to the stake, to the fagots, to the beasts, who saw their men, women, their little children, bruised, beaten, burned, torn asunder, and who counted it all a matter of deep and unselfish joy to pay, to seal, to witness with their lives their adoration, their consecration to Christ.

O brethren and sisters in Christ, compare that with the kind of Christianity we have today, that has to be begged, cajoled, implored, even so much as to attend worship regularly. Surely Christianity is a religion for heroes and heroines, and we, God help us, are not of heroic mold.

But even that is not all. Together with Paul, we are debtors to our contemporaries, to those who even now live all about us. We are debtors to our fellow-Christians. There never has been a time in the history of Christianity when the forces of evil have more and more definitely aligned themselves so forcefully against the armies of God. In every city and country, Christianity and Christians are battling for their existence. This is a time when the armies of Christ, convicted, consecrated, concentrated, soul to soul, heart to heart, mind to mind, life to life, blood to blood, and by the grace of God, are to beat and batter down the gates of hell.

We are debtors to a lost world all around us, on every hand, in every place. In every block, in multiplied multitudes of homes, there are souls without God, without Christ, without hope, souls steeped in sin, sold to Satan, straying into hell, consciously and unconsciously. They need our help. We and we alone have the keys of heaven.

Some years ago while this humble preacher was in the Seminary, the good Dr. O. L. Hailey, President of the American Baptist Seminary, Nashville, Tenn., told the evangelism class this matchless story:

It seems that in the inception of the seminary, when it was just a few months old, the school and he came into financial straits. He traveled to Texas to visit the home of a rich rancher with the purpose in mind of asking for a contribution or a loan. The rancher was a friend and kinsman. When Dr. Hailey approached him and asked for one thousand dollars the rancher at once drew out his check-book, filled out a check for that sum, signed it, tore it out of his book, and started to hand it to the preacher. Before the preacher took it, the rancher asked him what it was for. Dr. Hailey said, "It's for the work of my Negro seminary."

The rancher angrily withdrew the check, tore it into a hundred pieces, scattered it all over the floor, jumped up and cried, "What has a Southern gentleman to do with a bunch of cursed Negroes anyhow? If God wants to save those blasted Negroes, He will do it without you. I wouldn't give you two cents for the whole rotten lot of them!"

In spite of the appeal and protest of the seminary president, the rancher was adamant. Day after day the discussion went on. The cowman absolutely refused to take any interest in the matter. Sunday came. The rancher and Dr. Hailey sat on the front seat of a carriage, while the rancher's wife and father occupied the rear seat as they drove to church. Dr. Hailey had been praying with all of his soul that God might move the heart of this rich man to help in this desperate matter. As they drove along, the seminary president turned to his friend and said, "Jim, slow up. We've got plenty of time. I want to tell you a story.

"Some years ago a party of American emigrants traveled from New York to California. They got lost on the great American desert and ran out of water. The stock began to die, the children to cry, the women to whimper and moan, the men to grumble. The captain of the caravan was concerned about conditions, and early one morning, before sunup, sent scouts in every direction to search for water. One of them set out to the northwest. For hours he rode his horse without sighting water. Toward noon, as he topped a small sand dune, he saw what looked like trees in the distance, a little to the right of his course. Whipping up his horse, he sped towards it. It was an oasis around a spring that gushed out of a small rocky formation, forming a pool about the size of an average house. The man jumped off his horse and carefully watered it. He undressed, plunged into the pool, and soaked up the water with every pore in his skin. He swam to the spring and drank his fill. Coming out of the water, he dried himself, dressed again, filled his water bags, and canteens, took another long, thankful gaze, gave his horse a drink, got up into the saddle, and turned the animal back toward the party. The sandy expanse stretched out before him. There was no sign of any road. The shifting sand had covered his tracks, but he was plainsman enough to have easily found his way back. The sun was blazing now. He reined in his horse and said to himself, "It's a long way back and hard. There's nobody in that party who belongs to me. I know my way now. I will just go on and let the rest root for themselves."

The rancher placed his heavy hand clutchingly on Dr. Hailey's arm, "O. L.," he cried, "you know what I'd do with a man like that?"

"What would you do?"

"Why, I'd tie him to my buggy wheel and take a blacksnake whip and cut him to hell."

Dr. Hailey put his arm around the speaker. "Jim," he said, "What would you do to a man who had the water of life and refused to pass it on to sin-cursed, dying, hell-bound souls?"

Beloved, he got his check and many, many more liberal ones. So the seminary was saved, and the work went on. That is what I mean. In every direction from us, in every city, in every countryside, in every State are precious souls lost in the desert of sin. We know the oasis; we know the rock that was stricken for our salvation, from Whose side, from Whose hands, from Whose feet and head, poured the life-giving flow, even our Rock of Ages. Tell me, shall we stand idly by and drink of the fountain and ever hesitate to pass it on to others?

III. *I Am Ready*

Now, because we are not ashamed of the gospel of Christ, because we are debtors to Christ, to God, the conquerors of the past, our contemporaries, to every soul out of Christ. What is the very essence, the very heart, the very blood, the very soul of Paul's cry, we are *ready* to *live,* to live as Jesus lived, to live as Jesus would live were He in our shoes, in our homes, in our circumstances, in our activity. Regardless of what others may do, regardless of what others may ask us to do, regardless of any pleasure, regardless of any problems, regardless of any proposals, we are ready to live the Christ life. It may cost us wealth, ease, pleasure, health, our very lives, but as Christ was ready to die for us on the cross, we are ready to live the cru- cified life for Him. Beloved, that is the greatest need today—this readiness to live the New Testament life. It will do more, it will help more, it will serve more, it will win more, it will last longer, it will glorify Christ more, it will win more souls, bring more pressure, advance the kingdom farther, help the world more than anything and all things else we may be able to do. It cost Paul everything he was and had to say, "I am ready," and live up to it.

Beloved, apostolic succession demands that we are also to pay the same price. Christianity is a heroic religion, calling out, challenging, constraining with an imperial compulsion, the very best that is in us, the loftiest, the holiest, the honorable, the courageous, to live devout, undefiled, sacrificial Christian lives day by day, day after day. "I am ready to live" ought to be written in letters of fire across our hearts, our minds, our souls, our lives. It ought to be our prayer by day and our dream by night. We are ready to live because we are not our own, because we are bought with a price, the price of the blood of Christ. We are living on borrowed time, on gifted time, on time that belongs to someone else.

We are ready to give—to give our talents, our toils, our tears, our tithe, and all that we are and possess or ever hope to possess. Permit me to make an humble and yet burning suggestion. The next time you are called upon to make a contribution, whether in time or in money, before you make up your mind what it will be, how much it shall be, close your eyes, think upon Calvary's cross, see the pierced hands, the torn feet, the streaming, wounded side, the crown of thorns, take everything you are and have, stretch it out on the altar in the agony of abandonment. Even then, after you have done all that, if you can call it sacrifice, brother, sister, you need to tarry at the cross. Many have given—Peter, Paul, James, John, Huss, Savonarola, Latimer, Ridley, John Bunyan, Roger Williams, Adoniram Judson. We, too, by the grace of God, by the vision of Christ, by the impulsion of the Spirit, are ready to give.

We are ready to go, to go with weeping, sowing the seed, so that we may come back rejoicing, bringing our sheaves with us to deposit at the feet of Christ. Oh, the terrific need of going Christians! We have talented, trained, popular, influential, cultured Christians. We need going Christians, weeping Christians, sowing Christians, reaping Christians. We preachers must lead the parade; you deacons, stewards, elders, trustees, must come next; you Sunday-school officers, teachers, women's officers, young people's leaders, must close up the ranks. Like an army with invincible power, shoulder to shoulder, life to life, heart to heart, soul to soul, we must go afield to challenge, to combat the hordes, the hosts of hell.

Some of you know that when I was converted in 1925, my people turned their faces from me. I have no standing in the family circle. It is a hard, bitter cross of a thought, but there it is. In 1933 when I was pastor in Vickery, Texas, my father came from Chicago to see me, to take me home. He spent eight days with me, and I came closer to hell in agony of heart and soul during those eight days than I ever expect to be in time or eternity.

I took him off the train. We hugged and kissed each other, got into my car, drove home. On the way he told me about my precious mother, my four brothers, my sister, how much they loved me, how they wanted to see me, and began to ask me to give up my Lord and my work, to come home. I introduced him to my wife. He liked her and said so. I want him to like my wife and my children who have come since then. It is my prayer that somehow my family may be used of God to melt the hearts of my people and open the way for me to be with them.

During those eight days, by day and by night, I tried every way, I used every method to win my father to Christ, but to no avail. He refused even to look at a New Testament. He turned his back on my Christ. It broke my heart, and I was in deep soul agony. Night after night he would stretch out his old hands to me and, with tears streaming down his face, in a trembling voice, he would ask me to come home. Night after night I would be obliged to refuse. He would go to his bed, I would go on my knees or face, weeping my heart out.

Came the day of his departure. Together we sat in the Pullman seat. Again he plead with me to turn my back on Christ and the church and my humble work, to come home. He said, "Son, Mamma's getting old, I am getting old, you are our firstborn, we have done all we could for you, as sacrificially as we knew how. Won't you come home? We haven't much longer to live. Cheer our old age. I've got some money with me. I'll buy your ticket. Don't get off the train. We'll send for your wife. We've got plenty of money. Come home."

Again I had to say, "I can't, Father; it's impossible and out of the question."

He kept on pleading, the tears splashing on his old cheeks, every tear a drop of burning acid on my soul. He kept on begging, pleading, reasoning. After a while someone called, "All aboard." I knew I had to get off. I stood up. My father tried to stand with me, but I knew it was of no use, so I pressed him down into the seat. Bending down, I pressed my lips to his: "Daddy," I said, "this for Mamma. Tell her no matter how it seems, no matter how it looks, no matter how it appears, I love her with all my heart." Then I kissed him and said, "Daddy, this is for you. I love you more than you will ever know. Daddy, there is one thing I want you to know. Whether you can ever accept my way or not, whether you can ever agree with me or not, I want you to know that I am just as honest and sincere as I know how to be."

I jumped off the train, got into my car, and started to drive away, but the tears blinded me. Parking my car near the station, I bowed my head over the steering-wheel and poured out my heart to God that He might have mercy on my loved ones.

You turn to me, my beloved, and say, "Preacher, you love your people; why didn't you go? They needed you. They are getting old. They had sacrificed for you. Why didn't you go on home?"

I'll tell you why. All the time my daddy was weeping, all the time I was praying, all the time my heart was breaking, above his head I could see a hill, and on that hill a cross, on that cross the bleeding, broken body of my Savior.

Beloved, I may be a Jew, but I am not a dog! If Jesus Christ loved me enough to die for me, I love Him enough, and I want you to love Him enough, so that together we may be ready to live, to give, and to go. God, give us the grace to do it for Jesus' sake. Amen.

III

TAKING CHRIST'S PLACE

*Then the same day at evening, being the first day of
the week, when the doors were shut where the disciples were assembled for fear of the Jews, came
Jesus and stood in the midst, and saith unto them,
Peace be unto you. And when he had so said, he
showed them his hands and his side. Then were the
disciples glad, when they saw the Lord. Then said
Jesus to them again, Peace be unto you: as my Father
hath sent me, even so send I you. And when he had
said this, he breathed on them, and saith unto them,
Receive ye the Holy Ghost: Whose soever sins ye
remit, they are remitted unto them; and whose soever
sins ye retain, they are retained.*—John 20:19-23

YOU WILL consider these five verses as my text, stressing
especially the statement, "As my Father hath sent me,
even so send I you." This is John's report of the Great
Commission. You recall readily Matthew's statement,
"Go ye therefore and teach all nations, baptizing
them in the name of the Father, and of the Son, and
of the Holy Ghost," and the rest of it. You will recall
Mark's, "Go ye into all the world, and preach the gospel
to every creature." You will remember Luke's, "Ye
shall be witnesses unto me both in Jerusalem, and in all
Judea, and in Samaria, and unto the uttermost parts
of the earth." John's is the clearest, simplest, sweetest,

36

most definite, most direct. As you analyze it, clearly, unmistakably, there surge into your mind three thoughts that will make up the outline for this humble message. First, What did Jesus Christ come to do? Second, What does Jesus Christ want us to do? Third, How are we going to do it?

WHAT DID JESUS CHRIST COME TO DO?

Why did He leave His glory home in heaven to come down to this earth, to limit Himself in man's estate to suffer, to bleed, to die? That is the *mission* of Christ. What was it? Hear the Spirit tell it. Hear the words of Jesus:

"For God so loved the world that he gave his only begotten Son that whosoever believeth in him should not perish but have everlasting life." "God was in Christ reconciling the world unto himself." "He that hath seen me hath seen the Father." Jesus came on a mission of revelation. He came to reveal the person, the passion, the purpose, the program, the power of the Father. He came to show that God was not some far off potentate exercising despotic authority over his unfortunate subjects, but a father-hearted, compassionate, yearning, loving parent brooding over the children of His heart. He came to show that it was the purpose of God not to condemn but to save a world of men. He came to show that God was ready, eager, anxious to go to any length to help, to keep, to sustain, to provide for the safety and the well-being of every one of us. But that is not all. Step out farther into the Word of God.

"For the Son of man came not to be ministered unto but to minister, and to give his life a ransom for many." Jesus came on a mission of redemption. By

the blood-sweat of Gethsemane, by the lonely agony of
Calvary, by the cruel nails, by the sharp thorns, by the
Roman spearhead, by the spilled blood, He came to
redeem men from the slavery of Satan, from the wages
of sin, from the curse of the law, from the wrath of
God. In His own dear body, He bore all of our sins
that we might be made the righteousness of God in Him.
By His own cruel pains He freed us from the penalty
that the justice of God had recorded against us in the
books of eternity. He tasted the pangs of death that
we might live forevermore. He slept in the narrow grave
that it might form a doorway for us into glory. He
supped the bitter cup of hell that the burning pit might
be bridged over for us. But even that is not all. Come
a little farther. How read ye?

"The Son of man is come to seek and to save that
which was lost." "For it pleased the Father that in him
should all the fulness dwell; and having made peace
through the blood of his cross, by him to reconcile all
things unto himself . . . and you, that were sometimes
alienated and enemies in your mind by wicked works,
yet now hath he reconciled in the body of his flesh
through death, to present you holy and unblameable and
unreprovable in his sight." Jesus came on a mission of
reconciliation. Between us and God there stood the
barrier, the burden, the mountain, the river, the swollen
ocean of our sins. We were enemies of God, aliens to
the commonwealth of Israel. By His fearful death on
the cross, Jesus removed that burden, tunneled that
mountain, bridged that river, split that ocean. There
is a highway between us and the heart of God, a royal
way, a red way, the way of the blood-stained cross that
leads home to God and glory. By the awful work on

Golgotha's gory ground, Jesus provided for our reconciliation to God.

The mission of revelation is finished. Not one jot or
tittle can we add to it. Let a man be convinced that
Jesus is the Son of God, that He came into the world
to die for sinners. Let him follow Jesus in the wonderful ministries of His life. Let Him kneel in dark
Gethsemane. Let him face cruel Calvary. That man
will believe; he must believe that God is love, that God
is anxious for his soul's welfare, that God stands ready
to clasp him in arms of love.

The mission of redemption is finished. When Jesus
threw back His head against the cross, cried, "It is
finished," bowed His head and died, redemption was
completed. There remains no more to be done. The
crimson price has been paid in full. Sin, all sin, has
been atoned for. Were all the Christians of all the
generations to mingle their sacrificially spilt blood with
the blood of the Savior, it would not add a feather's
weight of value to the effectiveness of Calvary's bloody
shower.

Jesus does not need our help in that. He trod the
winepress of God's wrath alone. He needed no help
then. He needs no help now. He never shall need help
in the ministry of redemption.

The mission of reconciliation is unfinished. It is here
that Christ uses us. As long as there is an unsaved
soul anywhere in the world, as long as there is a slave
of sin who needs to know about the fountain that flowed
from Immanuel's veins, just so long is the mission of
reconciliation unfinished. That is the task to which
Christ calls us. We are to tell a dying, sin-cursed, Satan-
ridden, hell-bound world that there is balm in Gilead,
that there is peace at the empty tomb, that there is

pardon on Calvary. That is what Jesus Christ wants us
to do, to preach, to sing, to witness to the ends of the
earth, to bring Christ to men and men to Christ.

Consider then *what Jesus wants us to do,* or, in one
brief word, the *commission* of Christ. It is directed
to every one of us who names the name of Jesus as
Christ and Lord. There is no exception, no escape, no
excuse. The selfsame blood that washed away our sins
signed our commission, enlisted and enrolled us in the
great task of winning souls for Christ.

By the Word of the Master, we are to be the salt of
the earth with the tangy savor and flavor of Christ's
abiding presence exercising its pervasive, purifying,
preserving, taste-inducing influence in every sphere of
our activities. Our lives are to leaven the world for
God. None coming into contact with our personalities
and activities but are to feel the steadying, sanctifying,
sustaining presence of the Holy Spirit permeating
through us. Our activities must radiate a perfume that
will make men homesick for the gardens of glory.

By the appeal of the Redeemer, we are to shine as
the lights of the world, pointing blundering, wondering,
wandering souls out of the miasmic darkness of sin's
desolation into the glorious light of God's grace. All
about us a world is staggering in the darkness of
iniquity, in the stupidity of transgression, in the black-
ness of unbelief. Leaders they have, many and clamor-
ous, yet are they but the blind leaders of the blind. This
whole world is a prison cell, a slave dungeon, a squir-
rel's cage treadmill. Everywhere men are sighing for
release and relief. We know the way of the cross. We
are basking in the light of Calvary's beacon. Lighting
our souls, our hearts, our lives at the blazing conflagra-
tion of Golgotha, let us up, and out, and on, calling

to men, beckoning men, pleading with men, guiding men to the Sun of righteousness with healing in His wings.

By the command of the Lord, we are to be witnesses, testimony-bearers. We are to witness to the world that Jesus Christ is abundantly and super-abundantly able to save unto the uttermost all them that come unto God by Him, seeing He ever liveth to make intercession for them. We are to witness by our courageous, heroic, challenging, lofty living that this Jesus not only saves but keeps. With the brightness of God on our faces, with the joy of salvation bubbling up in our hearts, with the songs of the redeemed on our lips, with springing step and back-thrown head, let us march on to Zion. That will make men want to share the secret of our zest and zeal. Meditating in our minds, singing in our hearts, proclaiming with our lips, we are to tell the story again and again, in home, in school, in market-place, in factory, in office, everywhere men gather in this workaday world. Christ has commissioned us to be winners of men, fishers of souls. He has promised us all the power in heaven and on earth. He has guaranteed us His victory-bringing presence to the end of the world, to the end of the age. We shall not fear, nor faint, nor grow tired, nor become discouraged until we hear the welcome plaudit of Prince Immanuel, "Well done, thou good and faithful servant."

But, *how are we going to do all this?* How are we going to carry on and out the task of the Redeemer? We are so weak. We are so few. We are so small. The generations have swept by and on and out. There are more myriads without Christ today than there have ever been. Our talents are too meager, our powers too weak, our days too short, our weaknesses too many. Now, how

are we going to keep faith with Him who loved us and
gave His life for us? In just one way, in but one way,
in only one way is there hope for our success—in the
way of *submission* to Christ. Jesus said, "Follow me,
and I will make you fishers of men." Let us take Christ
at His word. To do that three steps are required.

First, there is to be the enthroning of Christ, the giving
to Christ of the first, the choicest, the best, the most valuable that we have. Someone has very aptly said, "You
do not crown Christ at all, if you do not crown Him
Lord of all." Therein is the secret of victorious living.
Great Christians were not born great. They did not have
greatness thrust upon them. One by one, in agony, in
self-denial, in self-surrender, in total oblivion to the
things of the world, the flesh, and the devil; toiling,
struggling, striving, up and up they climbed the steep
ascent to Victory. Treading in the bloody footprints of
their Great Example, they left many a drop of blood
to mingle with His. With Paul, they filled up the cup
of Christ's sufferings. There is no other way to lofty
Christianity, to successful service in the field of the
Master. It is all or nothing. Trifling, piddling, drib-
bling, all these may avail in other fields, although even
in them the guerdon goes to the single-minded, to the
stout-hearted, but in triumphant kingdom building, they
have no place. Give Christ the right of way in all
things, in all places, at all times. That is the first step.

Second, there is absolute dependence on the Holy
Spirit. Jesus knew the importance of that. He gave
the disciples no college or seminary course; He be-
queathed them no organization or set of rules; He bade
them tarry in Jerusalem until they were endued with
power from on high. The disciples learned that lesson
ably and well. Time and time again they returned to

the Lord in earnest, tarrying prayer for the refilling of their souls with the Holy Spirit. The ages of Christianity that have passed, the lives of the mighty servants of the cross that have passed on before us, are another demonstration of the need, the utter, absolute need of the Pentecostal experience of those who would win the fight against Satan in their own hearts and in the hearts and lives of others. The Holy Spirit is available. You may have Him now, today, this hour, this moment, if, O God, grant that this if may become indeed and in truth your experience, if you will let Him have you. God is ready, eager, anxious to pour out the fulness of His mighty power into and upon your soul, if you will enthrone Christ now and forever. That is the second step. Submit to God, surrender your heart, your minds, your life, your soul, your all. Stay on your face before God until the fulness of the Pentecostal tide sweeps and surges across your souls, endueing you with the power that is from above.

Third, each of us, personally, definitely, unassignably, inescapably, is to take his or her place in the ranks of the marching, fighting, winning armies of the cross. Regardless of age, of circumstances, of training, of personality, the Captain has a place, a task, a duty for each of us to perform. Some of us are to go to the ends of the earth, carrying the message of eternal life to those in the darkness and bitterness of heathen idolatry. Some of us are to stay by the stuff, giving of our prayers, of our means, holding the ropes. Some of us are to battle the enemy in the home lines, preaching, teaching, organizing, building. All are to give themselves to the task of holding aloft the cross of Him who said, "And I, if I be lifted up from the earth, will draw all men unto me." At home and abroad, in business, in pleasure, by day, by night, in season, out of season, precept upon precept, line upon line, here a little, there a little, as God gives us strength, as the Spirit gives us utterance, we are to bring the bread and water of life to those in the hunger and thirst of sin.

You say, "Preacher, it is easy for you to speak that way. You are college-bred, seminary-trained. Your work as an evangelist has given you the practice, the training that you need to carry on in this business. But with us, it is different. We are just run of the mill. We try to be good Christians. We try to live clean lives. We want to win souls, none better, none more anxious than we, but we just don't know how to begin." Permit me then to finish this humble message with an illustration that marked an epoch in my own Christian life.

I have a dear preacher friend, Oby Nelson, pastor of Royse City, Texas. We have been praying partners for many years. He told this story in a Baptist association meeting in Texas. When he was much younger, say, twenty years ago, Brother Nelson and another young preacher, John Skaggs, held a brush arbor meeting in one of the school communities on the Red River near Gainesville, Texas. People came. The Lord was with them. Souls were converted and baptized into the church. One day, after the morning service, a young man told Brother Nelson that Dummy Walker was coming to the mourner's bench that night for salvation. Now, Dummy was the deaf and dumb (born that way) son of a Baptist deacon of that community named Walker. Dummy had not missed a service of the revival, but of course he had not heard a syllable of the proceedings. The two preachers, Nelson and Skaggs, walked over to where dummy was standing by a buggy and accosted him.

"Dummy, do you know what it means to be a Christian? Are you ready to accept Christ as your Savior?"

Dummy opened his mouth, smiled widely, and made that awful, heart-rending sound that a deaf and dumb person makes when he tries to speak. It was clearly seen that Dummy neither understood the others nor could he make himself understood. Not willing to give up too easily, the two preachers placed Dummy in their buggy and drove over to his father's place. The old man was in the yard of his home, working on some harness, when they rode up.

"Mr. Walker, Dummy wants to give his heart to Christ, and we want to be sure he knows what he is doing. Will you try to explain to him the meaning of being saved?"

The farmer man looked out across his fields. His eyes filmed over with unshed tears. "Brother Nelson, and you, Brother Skaggs," he said, "I am fifty-three years old. Dummy is twenty-four. I have been a Christian and a Baptist since I was nine and a deacon for over thirty years. I can make that boy understand almost anything about the work of the farm, but I have never been able to explain Christ to him, and God knows I've tried. Perhaps his mother can; she is in the kitchen."

They walked into the kitchen. "Mother, Dummy wants to be saved. We do not want to stand in his way, but we want to be sure he understands what he is doing. Can you ask him some questions about his soul and his sins, also about the Savior?"

The mother covered her face with her apron and sobbed. After some minutes, her face streaked with tears, she turned to the preachers. "Brethren," she said, "I am forty-eight years old. I have been a Christian since I was eleven and a church-member all this time. I can make son understand almost anything about the house, but I have found it impossible to explain the plan of salvation to him. Perhaps his sister can make him see it. She is visiting from Sherman. She is in the garden."

The group walked out into the garden. "Sister," spoke Nelson; "Bud here wants to come into the church. We want to know if he understands the step he contemplates. Can you ask him some questions about Jesus Christ for us and make him understand?"

"Brother Nelson," said the sister, "I am twenty-seven years old. I have been a Christian and a church-member since I was eight. Ever since I was a little girl, I have brought picture cards from Sunday-school for Dummy. I've tried every way I know how to make him know about the Savior, but it just is no use. He doesn't seem to understand. Don't you reckon the Lord will take care of him anyway?"

"I do not know, sister," said the preacher, "but let's ask Him. Let us pray." The six of them got down on their knees in the garden. One by one the five normal ones lifted their voices to God for Dummy's soul. They then separated to their tasks.

That night the brush arbor was packed. The news of Dummy's problem had been broadcast over the countryside. Skaggs led the song service. Oby Nelson preached. When he gave the invitation, the first man to walk down the aisle was Dummy Walker. Nelson bowed his head in his hands and sobbed. The problem was beyond him. Dummy knelt at the mourner's bench. A deathly silence, broken only by muffled sobs, settled on the crowd. After some minutes the preacher felt a tug at his coat. Dummy, face lit up with an unearthly light, stood before him. The boy did not offer his hand as was the custom. Instead, he raised his two hands and made as though he were embracing the skies, then brought them down to his heart. He repeated the gesture, touching the Bible, touched his dusty knees, stretched out his hand to the preacher, and everybody in the crowd knew that Jesus had worked one more miracle and saved the deaf and dumb boy's soul.

Facing that Baptist Association crowd in Navarro County, Texas, Nelson finished his story. "Brethren and sisters," he said, "Dummy Walker won more souls to Christ during the remainder of that revival than any three of us." When the service was over and we all were out in the church yard, eating our association dinner, I questioned Oby further. "Oby, that surely was a great story, but, boy, didn't you put on the rousements at the end?"

"What do you mean, rousements?"

"Well, how could a deaf and dumb person lead souls to Christ?"

"That's all you know, Jew. Put your plate and cup down." I did, on the running-board of a near-by car. Oby did the same. He came up to me, put his arm around my shoulder, and spoke on.

"After the night of his decision, Dummy would do personal work in that crowd. He'd go up to an unsaved man or boy, put his arm about him, press him a little, point to his heart, point to his own heart, point to the heavens, point down the aisle, and gently compel them to the front."

Nelson and I left our lunches just where they were. We walked over to a barn almost filled with hay, burrowed into it, stretched out on our faces, and held a prayer-meeting. I do not know what Oby said. I was too busy getting right with Jesus about that time. When my friend had finished his prayer, I lifted my heart and voice to God, and this is what I said: "Lord Jesus, it is not in me to be a Paul. It is not in me to be a Wesley. It is not in me to be a Truett. But, oh, make me, oh, do make me a Dummy Walker. Let me use what You have given me for Your glory and the salvation of souls."

Brethren and sisters in Christ, that is my message to you. In Jesus' holy, precious name, take up the pleading, challenging, inviting, constraining appeal of the Lord Jesus Christ, "As my Father hath sent me, even so send I you."

IV

THE ULTIMATE QUESTION

Pilate said unto them, What shall I do then with Jesus which is called Christ? They all say unto him, Let him be crucified.—MATT. 27:22

THIS is the ultimate question in time and eternity. It is by far the most important one we shall ever have to answer. Answer it right, and all else is right; answer it wrong, and all else is wrong. It is a personal question. We cannot answer it for each other. There are mothers in this congregation who would gladly shed every drop of blood in their veins to decide this problem for their children in the right way. There are fathers in this congregation who would gladly suffer any sacrifice, endure any pain, if they could make this decision for their loved ones. It is, however, an altogether personal question.

It is a pressing question. There are some questions you do not have to answer, but this one you must. If you avoid it here, you will face it hereafter. There is no escape from it. You may as well realize this tremendous fact and not foolishly delay, neglect, or reject the implications of this query. God, grant that it may never leave you, that it may never lose you, that

49

it may keep pressing upon you until you come to the right conviction and conclusion.

It is a present question. You must, you can, and you will answer it before this service comes to its end. There is no side-stepping it. There is no pleading of neutrality. There is no avoiding it in any conceivable way. You face it squarely tonight. You will either decide for Christ or against Him. You will either walk out of this congregation with Jesus on the road to heaven or with Satan on the road to hell.

Because of the vital importance of this question, because of its eternal implications, may I press it upon your consideration from these three angles. First, who is this Jesus? Second, why should you do anything with Him? Third, what will you do with Him?

I. Who Is This Jesus?

He is not just another man, another teacher, another Jew, another priest, another ruler, another statesman, another reformer, another ethical culturist, another religious visionary. He is the Son of God. He is God encased in the flesh of the virgin-born Son of Mary.

He is the Son of God who loved you and died for your sins. The love of Christ, the passionate, pure, persistent love of Christ, ought to constrain every one of us to love Him in return. The agony death of Christ on the cross, the blood letting, the blood shedding, the heartache, the heartbreak of Calvary's cross, must move each of us toward Him with the deepest affection of our souls. This is what makes unbelief such a heinous crime. This is what makes rejection of Christ the sin for which there is no forgiveness, neither in time nor eternity. That He loved us and died for us should lead every sinner to an acceptance of Christ as Savior and every Christian to surrender to Christ as Lord and Master. That was the motto, the motive, the message of the apostle Paul. "The love of Christ constraineth us, because we thus judge, that if one died for all, then were all dead, and that he died for all, that they which live should not henceforth live unto themselves but unto him which died for them and rose again." That was the ultimate expression of the ministry of John the Beloved: "Herein is love, not that we loved God, but that he loved us, and sent his Son to be the propitiation for our sins." That is the very soul of the gospel: "For God so loved the world, that he gave his only begotten Son, that whosoever believeth in him should not perish but have everlasting life." This love the Holy Spirit offers to every one of you on the terms of the gospel. It is this love you must consider when deciding what you will do with Jesus, which is called the Christ.

He is the Son of God, Who loved you, Who died for you, Who alone can save you from your sins, keep you out of hell, admit you into heaven. To Him God has given the full, the only authority for salvation. It is as true today as it was back yonder in apostolic times that "neither is there salvation in any other; for there is none other name under heaven given among men, whereby we must be saved." Not even God can forgive the sins of a single soul without the mediatorship, the shed blood, the saviorship, the Name of the Lord Jesus Christ. Refuse Him, reject Him, neglect Him, and the fierce fires of an eternal wrath-filled hell will be your portion. Accept Him, and though your sins be as scarlet, they shall be as white as snow; though they be red like crimson, they shall be as wool. This Jesus can save you. He wants to save you. He will save you

this very hour if you will choose with the overtures of
His mercy. Refuse Him, and some day you will face
Him, no longer the tender, patient, pleading, inviting
Redeemer, but the stern, inexorable, inflexible Judge
and Executioner, the Arbiter of your eternal destiny.
Yes, this Jesus is a two-sided Christ. To those who believe, He is the compassionate, gracious, pitying, longsuffering Jesus of the healings of Galilee, the prayers
of Gethsemane, the blood of Calvary. To those who
live and die in unbelief, He is the sword arm of the
Lord, the warden of God's marches, the destroyer of
God's enemies. In answering the question, what will
you do with Jesus? dwell earnestly, attentively, even
anxiously on the eternal verity that Jesus will either
be your saving God or your condemning Judge.

II. Why Should You Do Something with Jesus?

There are a great many reasons. There is not time
nor space for all of them. I could very easily, very
definitely, very truthfully say, "Because you've got to;
you cannot help yourself. God puts you to the question, to the test. You cannot escape the quandary." But
that would be a slavish reason, a weak answer. To do
something with Christ because you are compelled to
is to make a tyrant of God, an unwanted guest of
Christ. No, the Lord will not force you to decide. He
will plead with you, press Christ's claims upon you,
present His love to you, but the decision must be yours,
free, whole-hearted, whole-souled, uncoerced. The Lord
will force no man into Christ. The Lord will drive
no man into heaven. However, there are three basic
reasons why all should do the right thing with Jesus.

First, you need Him. You need Him in life. You
need Him in death. You need Him at the judgment.

You need Him throughout an endless eternity. You need Him for the forgiveness of your sins. You need Him for the feeding of your souls. You need Him for the understanding of the Word, the will, the work, the way of God. You need Him in joy. You need Him in sorrow. You need Him when you are well. You need Him when some dread disease takes possession of your body. You need Him in business, in school, in politics, in the social circles. You need Him at home. You need Him abroad. You need Him from the moment of your birth to the hour of your death. You need Him when the family circle is unbroken. You need Him when the angel of death visits the bosom of your family to snatch away some loved one into the darkness and mystery of eternity. You need Him when the clods of earth fall heavily upon a dear coffined form as though each were dropped on your very hearts. Yes, with all the passion of my love for you, I plead with you to see how desperately, how definitely, how dependently you do need the Lord Jesus Christ in the trials, the troubles, the tests of life.

You need Him when your time comes to render your soul back to the God who entrusted you with it as a sacred stewardship. You need Him when the heavy-winged, sable-hued messenger of death comes to bring the warrant of God for you to quit this life and go out into eternity. You need Him when your eyes begin to glaze, when your limbs begin to stiffen, when you lose sight, hearing, motion, when the death dew appears on your forehead, and the death rattle in your throat, when your soul stares out into an uncertain eternity. If you have accepted Christ, you need not fear. He who loved you enough to die for you loves you enough to lead you through the valley of the shadow of death safely

by His side. But, oh, if you have rejected Christ, if
you have neglected His tender invitations to salvation,
if you are dying unsaved, the fearful horrors of those
last minutes! There is nothing waiting for you but

The wrath of Him whom your sins have offended,
And the night, the dark night of eternal despair.

It is a fearful thing to die out of Christ.

You need Him in eternity. You need Him in the
judgment. You need Him to shut the gates of hell and
to open the gates of heaven to you. To those of us who
are in Christ, the judgment holds no terrors. "We have
an advocate with the Father, Jesus Christ the righteous."
He will represent us. He will speak for us. He will
be our Counsellor, our Defender, our Lawyer. He will
plead our cases. God cannot; God will not refuse Him
the boon of our admission into glory. But, suppose you
do the wrong thing with Christ. Inevitably, unavoid-
ably, inescapably, you will face God in the judgment.
What will be your defense when you are asked, "Why
have you rejected Christ?" What argument, what alibi,
what discussion, what extenuating circumstances will
you advance to ameliorate the awfulness of the fact
that you lived in sin, that you persisted in sin, that you
died in sin, that you rejected the way out of sin, even
the Lord Jesus Christ? Truly you have no excuse that
can be or will be accepted in that court of final justice.
Naked, stripped of every reason, of everything on earth
so high sounding, so seemingly logical disputation, with
the burden, the barrier, the bondage of your sins spread
before the eyes of men and angels, with Christ a witness
against you instead of a pleader for you, where will
you be in that hour of fearful scrutiny? O brother, O
sister, flee to Christ tonight! Let His precious blood

wash away your black sins!   Retain Him as your
capable counsel, as your undefeatable advocate.   He
is offering His services to you in this hour.   By faith,
close with Him!

Second, He needs you. That is a joyous thought, an
inspiring challenge. The Son of God, the King of kings,
the Lord of lords, the Creator, the Preserver, the Sus-
tainer of all this universe, this Son of God, Who has
all the power, all the wisdom, all the authority of God
Himself, this same Jesus, Who could just as easily have
used the holy angels in the work of His heart, this
Christ, wants you, needs you, appeals to you to enter
into His magnificent service.   Were the president of
these United States to look into your face; were he to
say, "Men, women, children, fellow citizens, I need
your help to make America what it should be; your
beloved country needs your help," there is not a soul
but who would leap up in glad response and say to the
president, "Here am I, send me."   Tonight, Jesus Christ
comes to you and says: "I need you in My service. I
need you to help Me bring in the kingdom of God. I
need you to help Me build a better world. I need you
to win lost souls to a saving acceptance of the gospel."
Tell me, what is your answer to this Master? Will you
say right now, this very moment; will you say it
and mean it; will you say it and do it: "Lord Jesus,
I love You for first loving me. I love You for
dying for my sins on the cross. I love You for all
the many blessings You have bestowed upon me.
I love you for the heaven You are preparing for me.
I love You, Lord Jesus. I cannot do much, but I love
you and gladly want to help You. If You can use me;
if You can find some lowly place in Your service for
me; if You can use my poor, humble talents in some

corner of Your great kingdom, here am I, take me,
break me, mold me, fill me, use me." You need not be
afraid of your sins, of yourselves, of your shortcomings.
Jesus can forgive your sins, overcome your weaknesses,
supply out of the fulness of His inexhaustible treasures
whatever may be lacking in your serviceability, in your
effectiveness.

The Master has a place in His service for everyone
of you. There is not a boy nor a girl, not a man nor a
woman, anywhere in this great throng tonight whom
Jesus Christ cannot use. Do not hesitate for any
thought or consideration. Do not look to yourselves.
Do not look to others. Look to Jesus. All He seeks
is a glad surrender. All He wants is an emptied life.
All He asks is a faith-induced submission. Just heed
His call. Just turn your life over to Him. Just come
now into His salvation, into His service.

Third, others, all about you, your loved ones, your
friends, your neighbors, others need you as Christians.
"No man liveth unto himself, no man dieth unto
himself," is still the dictum of experience. The least
and the highest among us have spheres of influence.
You are either pointing, aye, leading souls to God
and heaven, or you are directing them to Satan and
hell. There is not a listener so rotten, so polluted,
so stained, so cursed of soul, so low in character, who would deliberately cause a single sinner to
stumble into hell over our lives, to be eternally lost.
But, O friends, unsaved friends, drifting, irresponsible
Christians, don't you see that by doing the wrong thing
with Christ you are permitting the devil to use you as
a stumbling-block, as a decoy to those whom he is
seeking to destroy? By rejecting Christ, you are help-
ing others to do the same. By neglecting Christ, you

are leading others into the same fearful road of un-
avoidable destruction. Think of this. Tonight perhaps
you are not a Christian; or you are a backslidden Christian, having dropped your cross somewhere along the
road. You drift on and on. Your influence against
Christ spreads out and out in ever-widening circles.
Perhaps at some future date you yourself come or
come back to the Lord. The Redeemer, because He is
so everlastingly longsuffering, welcomes you and saves
your soul, but these others, these men, these women,
these children, these whom you have touched day in
and day out, these, where are they? Some have died
and gone into hell. Others, following your bitter example, have become hardened in sin, with the blessed
gospel having no effect upon them. It is a fearful
thought that your delay, that your indecision, although
by God's grace has not sent you into the pit of burning,
has been used of Satan so terribly, so effectively to
drag others into hell. Brethren, sisters, God help you
to see that there is many a soul in torment tonight sent
there by a Godless father, a Christless mother, a prayer-
less wife, a Bible-less husband, a heedless brother, an
indifferent sister, a careless friend, or a loveless neigh-
bor. For the sake of these others all about you, each
of you should do the right thing with Jesus. Your example, your influence is asked for by Christ and by
Satan. One you must choose. Oh, what will your decision be? Eternity is standing still; the angels are
bending down from glory; the demons are looking up
from hell to see what you will do with Jesus.

Many of you have unsaved or backslidden loved
ones and friends. You may be waiting for them to
make the good decision before you take any stand.
That is exactly what the devil wants you to do. Two

wrongs no more make a right in the Christian sphere of conduct than they do in any other sphere of human activity. Do your part! Get right with God yourself! Let the Lord have your life! Then, when you are on the altar for God, wh₋n you have recognized the claims of Christ over your own life, pray, work for your loved ones' souls. The merciful Lord will answer your prayers in saving and consecrating them also. Do it God's way! Do it the Bible way! Throw no obstacles in the path of the Holy Spirit! Give Him your life that He may use it to answer your prayers! Father, mother, come to Christ, come into your church, then go back and win your blessed children. Husband, come to Christ, then go about to win your wife. Wife, let God have His way with you tonight; then ask Him for the soul and the salvation of your husband. Children, this one time you must not wait for your parents. They cannot decide your destiny. It is a personal matter between you and the Lord. Give yourselves to the Redeemer of souls. God will use your young lives to break the hearts of your parents and bring them also to the cross. There is not one but who can and will help others to find Christ, if you answer this question right.

III. WHAT WILL YOU DO WITH JESUS ?

We are back to the same question. What will you do with Jesus? As God gave me utterance, I have shown you who this Jesus was and is; why you must do something with Him. Now, what will you do with Him?

What will you do with Him, Christian? Will you give Him the right of way in your life? Will you enthrone Him as the Lord and Master of all you are and have? Will you give Him, as He gave for you, the best of your time, of your talent, of your money, of yourself, of your home, as much as you can of your loved ones? Will you consider Him in the morning, let Him guide you during the day, blessing Him, praising Him, serving Him whenever and wherever opportunities offer themselves? Will you be loyal to His cause, to His kingdom, to His church? Will you spend some time with Him each day in prayer? Will you seek to learn more about Him in the pages of His Book? Will you try to tell others about Him that they, too, might share Him with you?

Christians, give up the besetting sin that has robbed Christ of your lives and love, and dedicate your lives afresh on His holy altar. There are some of you who could magnify and glorify Christ by coming into the church in the community where you live, on transfer of membership. The church is the bride of Christ. In serving the church, you serve Christ. In serving the church, you serve a needy world. In serving the church, you invest your lives in the best possible, the most profitable way. The church needs you. Your membership is but of little use in some far-off place where you seldom, if ever, go. This is where you want God to bless you. This is where you expect God to answer your prayers. This is where you are looking to God to prosper you, to keep you and yours in health. If you should die in your present home, it is from this place that you look to God to take you to heaven. This is where your church-membership should be also. This is where you should be serving the Lord with all you are and have. Salvation is at best a one-sided affair. God gives and keeps on giving. We take and keep on taking. We owe Christ a great debt. At the very best, we can pay but little of it. Christian, will you do the right thing with Jesus?

What will you do with Jesus, my unsaved friend? He is in your hands this hour. Some day you will be in His hands. It will be too late then to answer this question. Jesus puts Himself at your mercy. You can crown Him or crucify Him. You can love Him or leave Him. You can receive Him or reject Him. You can believe on Him or turn Him down. You must decide. Tell me, nay, tell God, tell Christ, tell the Holy Spirit, tell the angels, tell the saints in heaven, tell the demons in hell, tell time, tell eternity, what will you do with Jesus which is called the Christ? The heavens are bending down to catch the sound of your answer. See, yon moon and stars have paused in their orbits to watch your decision. The recording angel of God has dipped his pen in the blood of Jesus and has lifted it out to hold it poised over the Book of Life. Tell me, unsaved friend, will this mighty angel write your name a child of God as tonight you come accepting Christ or will he sadly shake his head and write the fearful word "lost" on your record? The devil is marshalling all of his forces to cause you to deny Christ. You know God wants you to come to Jesus. You know Jesus died to provide your salvation. You know the Holy Spirit is inviting you to come. You know deep down in your heart you also want to come. The only one who does not want you to come is Satan. Oh, do not listen to him. Close your ears to his hellish suggestions. He means you evil! He seeks your destruction! Turn away from him and his sly whisperings. Exert your courage; exercise your wisdom; come to Christ! Let Him save you! Come to Him this moment!

Much depends on your decision. There is your own salvation. There is your influence. There are the multitudes of others whom you might induce to come to Christ. There is the matter of wasting your life with the devil when you might be piling up rewards by using it for Christ. Why hesitate? Why delay? Why put it off? Do you really believe that Jesus will be more ready or more able or more willing to save you tomorrow than He is today? You cannot believe that. Jesus wants you this very hour, this very moment. Do not wait until some dreadful accident, some fearful calamity, some heart-breaking experience drives you to God. Come willingly, lovingly, gratefully. God is waiting for you.

Some years ago, in one of the Gospel Missions in the city of Philadelphia, during a patrons' service, a well known lawyer stood up to testify as to how he became a Christian. He said that when he was about twenty-four years of age he married a beautiful, talented, exceptionally good Christian girl. He, himself, was more or less of an atheist, at least in practice, without regard for the Lord, the Bible, or the church. He tried in every way to break his young wife from her church-going, God-serving habits, but, thank God, to no avail. She grew, if anything, more devout, more zealous, more spiritual. After some years there came into their home a baby daughter, a flaxen-haired, blue-eyed gift from the Lord. When the girl was small, young, a child, the mother carried her about. They would go to Sunday-school and church together. They attended prayer-meetings, W. M. S. sessions, revival services, and many of the other worship and service hours conducted by the church. But when the daughter grew to be a young woman, the father took her in

charge. She was beautiful, cultured, talented, and the
father was inordinately proud of her. He would take
her to his clubs, on week-end trips, on yacht parties,
to dances, to night clubs, and to other places of gayety
and amusement. Bit by bit the father weaned the girl
away from the religious ways of the mother, much to
that dear woman's chagrin.

The father would lie in bed on Sunday morning and
chuckle sinfully as he would hear his wife talking to
the girl. "Doris, please get up and come to Sunday-
school and church with Mother this morning," and as
he would hear the answer of his child: "Mamma,
Daddy brought me in so late last night. I am so tired.
Mamma, if you'll forgive me this time, I'll go next
Sunday sure." Next Sunday it would be some other
excuse until the daughter hardly ever went to church
anymore.

The months and years sped past. The girl was
twenty. She was engaged to be married to a fine young
man. The wedding was set for the late fall. About
the middle of October, when it gets pretty cool in the
Pennsylvania mountains, a group of young friends of
that girl accompanied the two lovers on a trip to a
mountain lake, forty or fifty miles from the city. They
chartered a motor boat, got far out into the lake, and
had a great time. When the shadows of the evening
began to fall, they turned for the shore. There is always
a smart-aleck in one of those parties, and this group
was no exception. One of the young men began to
rock the boat. He tilted it a little too far, and it turned
over, dumping the whole crew into the water. They
were about a block from shore. They could all swim.
Not one of them was so much as bruised, but the water
soaked them to their skins. Instead of waiting until

their clothes dried off, they jumped into their cars and sped back against the cool, rushing night wind into Philadelphia. The next morning the girl complained of a headache. She stayed in bed. The doctor came and pronounced it a cold. The girl, however, did not improve. The doctor came every day. The father called in a specialist, who declared it a case of pneumonia. All that medical science could possibly do— careful nursing, choicest of medicines, carefully prescribed diet—was done for the young woman, but it just didn't help. On the eleventh day after she had gone to bed, the family physician came out of her room, walked into the lawyer's study, told him that the girl was dying and that only a miracle could save her life. The doctor asked the father whether he wanted to tell the girl the terrible fact himself or whether he wanted the doctor to do it. The man said, "I'll tell her."

He walked into the sickroom, sat down heavily in the chair by the side of his daughter's bed, took her hand in his, and began to pat it. Many minutes went past before he could get up enough courage to tell the girl that she was dying, but finally he broke the fearful news to her. The mother began to weep silently. The girl threw herself toward her father.

"Daddy," she sobbed, "I don't want to die! I can't die! Daddy, I'm not ready to die! Daddy, you've got a lot of money. Isn't there anything you can do to keep me from dying?" She tried to raise herself out of bed, but Father and Mother held her down. For some minutes she cried wildly, then calmed down somewhat. She turned to her mother.

"Mamma, I guess a person has to die sometime, and this is just my turn. Mamma, do you think it would be bad taste for me to be buried in my wedding-dress?"

"No, darling," said her mother, biting her lips to keep from weeping. "I guess it will be all right if you want it that way."

"Mamma, do you think Ralph [that was her fiancé] would mind if I wore our engagement ring away?"

"No, darling, I do not believe he'd mind if he knew you wanted it that way."

The girl and mother kept on talking soberly, softly. The girl's voice grew weak, hoarse with the approach of death. She turned to the father, bowed over with his head in his hands.

"Daddy, before I go, there is one question I must ask you. Daddy, please tell me the truth about it."

"Go ahead, darling, I'll do the very best I can to answer you."

"Daddy, you've been saying all this time not to worry too much about religion. You've been saying that if I am a good girl, live right, follow the dictates of my conscience, heaven would take care of itself. Mamma has been telling me all these years that if I wanted to be with God when I died, I would have to take Christ as my Savior. Daddy, now I am dying, please tell me, whose way shall I take, yours or Mamma's?"

The man said he threw himself on his child, picked her up in his arms, almost out of bed, pressed her to his heart and told her: "Darling, if you have a moment to spare, for Christ's sake, for your own sake, for Mother's sake, for hard-hearted Daddy's sake, take Mother's way."

He said that by the time he lowered his daughter into bed, she was dead. As he testified, he stepped out into the aisle in his deep agony, pulled at his grey hair as if he were trying to tear it out, and in a voice of terrible emotion, cried out: "Brethren and sisters, only God knows whether my darling had time enough to take Mother's way."

But, O beloved, you have time enough to take Mother's way, to take Mother's Christ. Your very minds respond to the truth of the plea. Your hearts ring with the tenderness of the appeal. Your souls are moved with the constraint of the invitation. The pierced hands are tugging at your very beings. The Holy Spirit is pulling at every fiber of your make-up. Come to Christ. Say:

I will arise and go to Jesus,
  He will embrace me in His arms,
In the arms of my dear Savior,
  Oh, there are ten thousand charms.

V

SOUL SUICIDE

How shall we escape, if we neglect so great salvation; which at the first began to be spoken by the Lord, and was confirmed unto us by them that heard him?—HEB. 2:3

EVERY time I read this verse of Scripture, every time I try to preach on it, there comes to my mind an incident that happened long years ago before I became a Christian. It was about six in the evening, when a farmer, a young fellow, was walking from the village where he had bought some supplies, along the right-of-way of the Pennsylvania Railroad. It was getting dark—not quite dark—just in the gloaming. His arms were loaded with packages. He carried a lantern in his hand. Suddenly he stumbled, fell, and almost dropped the lantern and packages. Somehow he retrieved himself and looked down. Either by accident or on purpose, three of the ties had been pulled out and a great section of rail had been bowed out. The man knew if the train ever hit the bent rail, there would be a terrible accident. He also knew that at that time of the night the express trains—not one but several, for if you know New York and Philadelphia you know it takes more than one train to get the people from Philadel-

phiā to New York to their daily work and back again—
came thundering down the track. He did not have any
tools, and if he had it would not have done any good.
The job was too big for one man. He began to feel
the shaking of the road-bed. He could hear the blowing
of the whistle. The train was coming. He knew he
had but a few minutes to do something. He lighted the
lantern, dropped his bundles by the side of the track,
and started running down the track. The train kept on
coming toward him as he continued running toward it.
He ran just as hard as he could, looking ahead at the
train. He stumbled, fell, and smashed the glass of his
lantern. There wasn't anything more he could do. The
train was coming, the headlight blazing. God gave him
an idea. He kept on running, and just about the time
he and the train met, he jumped off the track and threw
the broken lantern into the face of the engineer in the
cab. They do not have fool engineers on the Pennsylvania Railroad. When the engineer saw the lantern,
he knew there was something wrong. He put on his
brakes and stopped about a block away from the
bowed-out track. That farmer got a Carnagie Medal.

The Holy Spirit is lifting up the cross of Calvary,
the broken, blood-stained body of Jesus. He is throw-
ing it in front of us. If you keep on this way, there
isn't anything ahead for you except death and damnation. "Stop! Look! Listen!" is what the Holy Spirit
is saying by this question, "How shall we escape, if
we neglect so great salvation?"

Analyze this question in your own mind as you
follow me. First, the great salvation. Second, how
people neglect it. Third, what will be the outcome of
such neglect. There are a great many reasons why this

salvation is great. I have not time to give all of them, but let me press three home to your hearts as the Holy Spirit gives me utterance.

First, it is a great salvation because of the fearfulness of its cost. Come with me to Calvary; stand in the shadow of that cross; look up into the agonizing face of Christ; once more listen to the drip, drip, drip, dripping of the life blood shed for your sins and mine. That is the price God paid to redeem us from our sins. Salvation is free, but it is not cheap. It cost more than all the riches of the universe put together. It cost more than all the rest of the treasures, the precious jewels, the powers, the stores, and the wealth of God put together. When God nailed His Son to the cross to pay the price for our redemption, He beggared Himself. God emptied Himself because He had given Christ, the dearest, the most expensive, the most costly, the very best He had to give. He gave His own heart to bleed out its drops of blood in our behalf. When you realize that, when you understand that, it makes a good Christian of you. You don't have to be begged to come to prayer-meetings. You don't have to be begged to give your money. One good, long, steady look at the Lord Jesus will make you serviceable. One look into the face of the Son of God will make you sacrificial. One long look at the broken, blood-stained body, will make you more than anxious, more than willing to show your gratitude, your appreciation to that dying Son of God by your efforts, your desire to do His will.

One good, long, steady look at the cross, my unsaved friend, and, if you have a single drop of gratitude in your heart, it will constrain you to come to Christ, to accept Him as your Savior, to be baptized, to enter into His service, to give your life as devotedly to Him as He gave His for you on the cruel, cursed cross. The costliness of that salvation is one of the mightest inducements to draw us to its terms and conditions. The costliness of that salvation is probably among the chief reasons why unbelief is such a terrible sin, the worst of all sins. Ingratitude, dire, bitter, black ingratitude is put to the charge of those who reject the offer of God's mercy in the blood of His Son. Let the price that was paid for your redemption break your hearts and melt your souls.

Second, it is a great salvation because of the fulness of its contents. In this great salvation, God offers to us all that we need to take care of the past, to provide for the present, to supply the future. It begins with the unlimited pardon of our sins and ends with the bliss of an eternal heaven. Our sins are washed away in the blood of the cross. Our needs are provided for in the promises sealed by the cross. The Holy Spirit is given to us because when the crucified Redeemer ascended on high after Calvary's tragedy and triumph, He led captivity captive and gave gifts unto men. By the cleansing blood, we are adopted, sealed children of God, the Father Himself making Himself totally, absolutely, eternally, effectively, providingly, victoriously, joyously responsible for every physical, mental, moral, social, religious, spiritual part of our lives and the lives of those we love, for whom we are responsible. There is no need for the believer to worry about anything. "He that spared not his own Son, but delivered him up for us all, how shall he not with him also freely give us all things?" "If ye, then, being evil, know how to give good gifts to your children, how much more shall your heavenly Father give the Holy Spirit to them that ask him?" The Father will walk with us, talk with us, guide us, instruct us, inspire us, encourage us, enlighten us in His will and way, giving us the grace to do His blessed work. Then, when our life of affliction is ended, when we have come to the end of the way, when at twilight we stand on the brink of the chilly Jordan, with its cold waters laving our feet, the Father will be there to guide us safely through the valley of the shadow of death into the light of the new morning. Oh, the greatness, the fulness, the completeness of such salvation!

> *Come ye sinners, lost and hopeless,*
> *Jesus' blood can set you free,*
> *For He saved the worst among you,*
> *When He saved a wretch like me.*
>
> *To the faint He giveth power,*
> *Through the mountains makes a way;*
> *Findeth water in the desert,*
> *Turns the night to golden day.*
>
> *In temptation He is near thee,*
> *Holds the powers of hell at bay,*
> *Guides you in the path of safety,*
> *Gives you grace for every day.*
>
> *He will keep thee while the ages*
> *Roll throughout eternity,*
> *Though earth hinders and hell rages.*
> *All must work for good to thee.*
>
> *Oh, I know, yes, I know,*
> *Jesus' blood can make the vilest sinner clean,*
> *Oh, I know, praise God I know,*
> *Jesus' blood can make the vilest sinner clean.*

Third, this salvation is great because of the freeness of its conditions. Despite the fearfulness of its cost, despite the fulness of its contents, this mighty, this matchless, this magnificent, this multifarious salvation is offered freely to the children of men. Without money and without price is the price-tag attached to the gift of God's love. Search the Bible, scan its pages, study its declarations! In every conceivable way, in every possible appeal, in every appealing form, the Lord proffers the blood of His Son, the salvation of our souls, to us. Hear Isaiah: "Ho, every one that thirsteth, come ye to the waters, and he that hath no money; come ye, buy and eat; yea, come, buy wine and milk without money and without price . . . . Seek ye the Lord while he may be found, call ye upon him while he is near; let the wicked forsake his way, and the unrighteous man his thoughts; and let him return unto the Lord, and he will have mercy upon him; and to our God, for he will abundantly pardon." Hear Jesus: "Come unto me, all ye that labor and are heavy laden, and I will give you rest!" Hear John: "And the Spirit and the bride say, Come. And let him that heareth say, Come. And let him that is athirst come. And whosoever will, let him take of the water of life freely." These are the words of God. Come, take freely, without money and without price.

The poorest and the richest, the youngest and the oldest, the weakest and the strongest, the Jew and the Gentile, the man, the woman, the child, all of us are on the same level, in the same need, in the same way, facing the same conditions when we come before God. God is no respecter of persons. The condition upon which salvation is granted to us is as enduring as the stars, and more so. Thank God for that. We all can and do know what we must do. The gates of mercy are as ajar to one as to another. Repentance toward God and faith in the Lord Jesus Christ are the two steps we must take to escape from the penalty of sin into the pardon of God, from the torments of hell into the triumphs of heaven. That is a price all may pay. Those are conditions with which all may comply. God has made them so simple that a child needn't err in pursuing them, that the wayfarer, though a fool, may read and understand. There is no obstacle, no barrier, no difficulty, no trial, no problem in any of our lives that need keep us from God when the offer of salvation is made to us on such free conditions.

Considering the fearfulness of the cost, the fulness of its contents, the freeness and simplicity of its conditions, beloved, is it not startling that so many hesitate, that so many refuse, that so many reject, that so many neglect that offer of God? I believe the angels of glory have difficulty in understanding the folly of human beings in turning their backs on the love of God. Yes, there are multitudes who fail to avail themselves of the tenderness of God's mercy, who live on in their sins, die in them, bear them in the flaming pit of an eternal hell forever and forever. Why? There are many reasons, but the three commonest, I believe, are iniquity, insensitiveness, indecision.

Iniquity has hold of some people. There is some sin in their lives they will not let go. D. L. Moody said that there are but two reasons that kept a soul from Christ, one or both. They are moral cowardice or some besetting sin. This sin need not be very great. Some nights ago, in a service, I went back to a young woman to speak to her about her soul. She told me very definitely she wanted to be a Christian but said, "Not tonight." After some pressure she admitted that the thing standing in her way was her dancing. She liked to dance, and she knew it would be frowned on (God

grant it be so always) in the church. She was willing
to take a chance with her soul, with her Savior, with
Satan, with heaven, with hell, for the bare pittance
of a dance. Shades of Judas! Talk about selling Christ
for thirty pieces of silver! It may be some greater sin.
Sins are numberless. The devil has plenty of them
with which to tempt the human heart, with which
to delude the human soul from an acceptance of
Christ. It may be crookedness in business, dis-
honesty in politics, social impurity, anything, everything. Beloved, you will agree with me, Christian and
unsaved, that there is no sin, aye, there are no sins in
all the world worth trading for the soul's salvation and
the eternal mansions in glory. There is not enough
in value the devil, the world, the flesh can offer
to any of us that would compensate for the wrath of
God's visitation upon us throughout an endless eternity.
Whatever your sin or sins may be, bring them in humble
penitence and confession to Christ. He will forgive
you for the past and give you power and grace to
overcome for the present and future.

Insensitiveness claims the souls of some folk. They
do not come to church very often. They read their
Bibles almost not at all. They do not give the Holy
Spirit a chance at their souls. They lack conviction,
deep, pungent, earnest conviction for sin, and the need
of the Lord Jesus Christ. They compare themselves
with church-members, with each other, with the people
about them who are more wicked than they are. They
minimize their own faults and maximize their own vir-
tues. Because they are not rank, raw, rugged sinners, because they are not guilty of the more carnal transgressions, because they have social standing, worldly reputation, because they are not drunkards, gamblers, racke-

teers, jail-birds, they do not feel their desperate need of a Savior. Regardless of your feelings in the matter, they, together with you, are lost in sin, on the road to hell, without God, without hope in the world, if you have not repented of your sins and very definitely, very personally, very publicly accepted Jesus Christ as your personal Savior. It is written in God's Word, "Except ye repent, ye shall all likewise perish." "Except ye be converted and become as little children, ye shall in no wise enter the kingdom of heaven." "Except a man be born again, he cannot see the kingdom of God." "He that believeth not is condemned already because he has not believed on the name of the only begotten Son of God." "Without the shedding of blood is no remission." Feel it or not, believe it or not, admit it or not, you need Christ Jesus. Insensitiveness, indifference, will not help at all.

Indecision is the direst trap of Satan. There are more people brought down into perdition by indecision than by any and every other trick the devil uses. He knows our frames, he recognizes our inclinations. He is brilliant enough to know that he cannot start us on the road into sin by some terrific act of transgression. As a matter of fact, he does not need to do it. He does not need to make us vile, wicked sinners. If he can get us to put off the matter of salvation long enough, he has us just where he wants us. Somewhere there is a story told of a preacher who dreamed that he died and went to hell. He found himself in the very throne room of Satan. Beelzebub was sitting on his throne, while before him at a horseshoe table were gathered all the demons in solemn conference. The devil was speaking to them.

"You are not working hard enough. We are not

dragging down as many souls. Those preachers in
churches are turning too many to Christ. You must
do something about it and speedily."

Hell grew as quiet as the city of the dead. The
demons looked at each other. One of them sprang to
his feet and said, "Your Majesty, let me go up there
to where that Jew is preaching. Let me walk up and
down the aisles to tell the people that the Bible is a lie
from cover to cover and that Christ is absolutely false."

The devil looked at him.

"Sit down. That trick has run its course. Every
person in that crowd believes the Bible to be the Word
of God and Christ the real religion. You had better
think up something else."

Again the pit grew silent. Another demon stood to
his feet. The devil recognized him. "Your Majesty,
let me go up there. I'll tell them that they are too
wicked to be saved, that Christ doesn't want to save
them; that they have sinned away their day of grace."

"You sit down, too," said the devil. "They read in
the Bible the invitations and promises of God. The
Holy Spirit is warmly pressing upon their hearts the
invitation of Christ. They know Jesus will save them.
You cannot trap them that way."

Again a stillness settled on the abodes of torment.
Minutes slipped past. The devil and his minions sat
in deep cogitation. Suddenly there sprang to his feet
one of the largest of the imps. "Your Majesty, I know
how we can fill the chambers of hell. I'll go up there.
I'll walk up and down that congregation. I'll stand
by the side of those sinners. I'll tell them, 'You are
lost. You are going to hell. Christ died for you. He
can save you. You need to go to heaven.' "

The devil rose to his feet. "If you tell them that," he cried, "they will all come to Christ."

"Wait," said the other. "When I get through telling them all that, I'll whisper, gently, softly, insinuatingly, 'What is the hurry? Put it off. Not tonight. Wait until the revival is over. Some other time. Not tonight.' "

Beloved, if you were to let the voice of God die out of your ears, you could hear the voice of the demons saying, "What is your hurry? Not now. Put it off." Oh, I beseech you, by the mercies of God, by the blood of Christ, by the appeals of the Spirit, by the fires of hell, by the joys of heaven, heed not Satan's emissary. Hear the voice of God as He cries to you, "Behold, now is the accepted time: Behold, now is the day of salvation." "Today if ye will hear his voice, harden not your hearts." God says now; the devil says no. Heed the Lord and be saved lest the gates of mercy be closed against you; lest the time of your preparation be ended; lest the patience of God be exhausted.

Permit, then, this last question: How shall you escape if you neglect this great salvation? You know you have sinned. You know your record is stained with your transgressions. You know you cannot save yourself. You know you must die. You know you must face God in the judgment. You know that to escape from hell and enter into heaven, you must avail yourself of that salvation. But, suppose you neglect it? Supposing you go on and on indefinitely, hesitating, refusing, delaying, supposing you die unrepentant, unconfessed, unforgiven? How shall you escape?

There is no escape for God. He must punish you. His law is unchangeable, immutable as the stars forever and ever. He can play no favorites. He can make no exceptions. As you lived, so shall you die; so shall you face the judgment. The wages of sin, the curse of the law, the wrath of God, the condemnation of a holy justice must be visited upon you, or God is no more than a weak, pusillanimous bogey-man. The very pillars of eternity, the very foundations of the universe, the very essence of God, cry for your condemnation. There is no escape for God.

There is no escape for you. You cannot put off the death angel. You cannot hide from the judgment. You cannot deny your sins. You cannot pay the forfeit without plunging into hell. No argument, no excuse, no alibi, no consideration of any sort or description will obviate the fact that you have transgressed God's law and denied God's Son. In the awful nakedness of exposure, with the mass of your sins piled high about you, with the stern record of your transgressions bared before God, there is no escape for you, my unsaved friend, if you reject Christ. Even Jesus will be your enemy. Even the Holy Spirit will be your accuser. Even the very choicest of your loved ones and friends will be compelled, heartbrokenly, to witness against you. The blood that alone could have washed away your sins will cry aloud your neglect, your disobedience, your refusal. "He that despised Moses' law died without mercy under two or three witnesses: of how much sorer punishment, suppose ye, shall he be thought worthy, who hath trodden under foot the Son of God, and hath counted the blood of the covenant, wherewith he was sanctified an unholy thing, and hath done despite unto the Spirit of grace? For we know Him that hath said, Vengeance belongeth unto me, I will recompense, saith the Lord. And again, The Lord shall judge his people." There is no escape for you.

Thank God, there is an alternative. You are still

in the time of grace. You are yet in a savable condition.
The hands of God are stretched out to you. The blood
of Christ is available for you. The Holy Spirit still
invites you. You may be saved with an everlasting
redemption. The matter is in your hands. The decision
is yours to make. God has done all He can do. Christ
has done His part; has done it well. The Holy Spirit
is pleading for your soul with all His might. The
answer is yours. Will it be sin or salvation? Will it
be Satan or Savior? Will it be God or the curse? Will
it be life or death? Will it be heaven or hell? Neglect
is refusal. Neglect is rejection. Neglect is defiance.
Neglect is destruction. Neglect is death. Neglect is
hell. This moment may determine your eternity. Will
you repent of your sins, put your faith in Christ, confess Him as your Savior before men?

Some years ago Daniel Curry, a Methodist circuit
rider, lost his way on the Nebraska prairies. The night
came. It was too late to go much farther. Curry dis-
mounted, unsaddled and hobbled his horse, built a little
fire, cooked the little supper he wanted, arranged his
saddle blanket and saddle, and prepared to sleep. By
the light of the fire, he read his Bible, lifted his heart
and soul to God in prayer, loosed his clothes, stretched
out on the blanket, pillowed his head on the saddle,
and slept. He dreamed that he died and that his soul
knocked on the pearly gates of glory. The angel opened
the gates and asked his name and reason for being
there.

"My name is Daniel Curry," answered the preacher.
"I have come to claim the mansion in the sky that Jesus
promised me long years ago."

The angel leafed the pages of a book on the table
by his side. "I am sorry," he said, "but your name is

not in this book. There is no place for you in heaven."

"I don't care whether my name is in your book or not," spoke Curry. "I know it is in the Lamb's Book of Life, and I am coming into heaven."

"Do you want to argue it out with God?" asked the angel.

"No," said Curry, "not unless I have to. But if you will not let me in any other way, take me to God."

"Stand still," said the angel. He stepped to Curry's side, put his hand under Curry's armpit, spread his mighty wings, and with a rush, soared up into the air bearing Curry with him. On and on flew the angel with the speed of thought. Curry kept his eyes open against the rushing wind. Suddenly he began to see a blazing, brilliant light, as of a thousand suns rolled into one. It blinded him. He closed his eyes to the glare. The angel sped for the very heart of that illumination. Suddenly he stopped and gently lowered himself and Curry to the pavement. The preacher looked down. He was standing on something that resembled crystal glass. He looked up. There on a white throne, high above him, sat one like unto the Ancient of Days, even Jehovah. Curry was stricken with terror. He was face-to-face with God. His knees gave way, and he prostrated himself on the ground. From the figure on the throne came a voice—stern, clear, solemn: "Who art thou; what seekest thou?"

Curry tried to rise, tried to speak, but fear had entered into his very bones. He could neither move nor utter a word. Again came the voice: "Who art thou? What doest thou here?"

Unnamable dread, horrible fear took possession of Curry's soul. His strength was gone. His mind refused to work. His lips were sealed with the awfulness of the Presence he was facing. Again came the dread speech. "Speak, mortal. Who art thou? What seekest thou?"

Just as the preacher felt that hell itself was yawning at his feet, there came the sound of sandaled feet, the soft murmur of cloth rubbing against cloth. Someone came to his side, bent over him, lifted him to his feet. An arm stole across his shoulders with the hand placing itself on his left breast. He looked over at it and saw a diamond-shaped scar. Daniel Curry knew it was well with his soul. From the majestic figure on the throne came the repeated question: "Who art thou? What doest thou here? What seekest thou?"

The figure at Curry's side spoke, gently as the summer breeze, sweetly as the lullaby of a mother to a sleeping child, tenderly as the cooing of the turtledove in the land. The words flowed up: "Father, this is Daniel Curry. Whatsoever sins he has committed, whatsoever transgressions may blot his record, whatsoever iniquities may stain his past, charge them all to Me. Daniel Curry confessed Me before men, and I am now confessing him before Thee, my Father in heaven."

Beloved, it may not be just that way, but the Bible says, "Whosoever, therefore, confesseth me before men, him will I confess also before my Father which is in heaven." Come accepting and confessing Christ, and from now throughout an endless eternity you may rest assured that you are God's in Christ.

VI

SCRIPTURAL CHRISTIANITY

And he said to them all, If any man will come after me, let him deny himself, and take up his cross daily, and follow me.—LUKE 9:23

SCRIPTURAL Christianity is the greatest need of the day in every way and in every place—Scriptural Christianity—not the brand of Christianity most of our church-members have, but Scriptural Christianity; not the Christianity that social gospel people would have us practice, but Scriptural Christianity; not the Christianity you can put on on Sunday morning when you go to Sunday-school and church and take off when you get home, to hang up until next Sunday.

First of all, Scriptural Christianity denotes possession. Show me a Christian, living the Bible, and I will show you a person who has Scriptural Christianity. Show me a person, no matter how long he prays, how well he looks or how loudly he shouts, who doesn't live out the practices, the precepts of the New Testament, and I shall show you a person who is not in possession of Scriptural Christianity. Living out Scriptural Christianity shows that you have the religion of the Lord Jesus Christ, that you are

81

born again, that you have been washed in the blood, that your name is written in the Book of Life.

Then Scriptural Christianity assures possession. It assures it to ourselves. If you were to ask me, "How do you know that you are a Christian?" I should say I know I am a Christian for two reasons. First, because the Bible says so, and second, my life (to God's glory and praise) is aimed toward God and heaven. I hate the things I once loved, and I love the things I once hated. I am trying to serve the Lord Jesus Christ. I am trying to deny the world, the flesh, Satan, trying to obey my Redeemer, longing in my heart to satisfy my Master. That is Scriptural Christianity.

Scriptural living assures our possession of salvation to others. With our lives reflecting the Christ, our actions illustrating the indwelling Spirit, our conduct exemplifying the gospel experience, others are constrained to know we have been with Jesus. Our lives become epistles of righteousness "known and read of all men."

Scriptural Christianity deepens possession. We need that. Not only does it denote possession, assure possession, but it deepens possession. You know, after all, there is just one way to get what we call feeling in Christ, in Christianity, in the church, in the service of the Lord, in our religion. There is just one way to get feeling and that way is by service. There is just one way to be a happy Christian; there is just one way to be a joyous, shouting, singing, praying Christian, and that is by service. By service! No matter how often you may lisp it to yourself, the Doctor Coue shibboleth, "Day by day in every way I am getting better and better," will not work in Christianity. You must take that religion and live it out.   When you live it out, it sends a song through your heart, your soul, your mind, your life.   You know you have it.   You show to the world you have it.   That wonderful feeling deepens, throbs, sounds, rings in your entire being.

But, what is Scriptural Christianity?   To tell you the truth, I don't exactly know, but this I do know; I know how it works.   I know what it does.   I have seen it work.   I have seen it in action, and you know they say, "An ounce of example is worth a ton of precept," or "An ounce of example is worth a storehouse of advice."   Now, Scriptural Christianity works out in three ways.

First of all, if you have Scriptural Christianity, you are going to be a saint.   Now, a saint is a twofold kind of person.   First, a saint is a saved person, a man or woman or child who has accepted Christ Jesus as his personal Savior, who has repented of his sins, who has put his faith in the Son of God, who has had the application of the blood of Jesus, who has been regenerated by the Holy Ghost.   You know what I mean.   I do not have to dwell on that much.   Now, that is God's part.   There is just one thing we can do to be saved, and that is to accept the salvation of God as the free gift of God's love.   We can't *make* ourselves saved.   We can't *study* ourselves saved.   We cannot *exercise* ourselves saved.   We .cannot *trouble* ourselves saved.   We cannot *toil* ourselves saved.   We cannot *give* ourselves saved!   But, thank God, we can *take* ourselves saved!   That is God's part.   We have little to do with it except as we come humbly and penitently to the feet of Christ, to the cross, and cry,   "Lord, have mercy on me, a sinner."

But the second part of that sainthood applies to us.

Not only is a saint a saved person, but he is separated. Not only is the Scriptural Christian saved, but he is separated. He is separated from the world, the flesh, and the devil. He is separated to God, to Christ, to the Holy Spirit, to the church, to the kingdom, to the Great Commission, to the service of fellow Christians, and to the service of the lost world all around. A Scriptural Christian is separated. That is what Paul, the apostle, meant when he said, "I beseech you therefore, brethren, by the mercies of God, that ye present your bodies a living sacrifice, holy, acceptable unto God, which is your reasonable service. And be not conformed to this world: but be ye transformed by the renewing of your mind, that ye may prove what is that good, and acceptable, and perfect, will of God" (Rom. 12:1-2). That is what the writer of Hebrews meant in the twelfth chapter when he said, "Wherefore, seeing we also are compassed about with so great a cloud of witnesses, let us lay aside every weight, and the sin which doth so easily beset us, and let us run with patience the race that is set before us, looking unto Jesus the author and finisher of our faith; who for the joy that was set before him endured the cross, despising the shame, and is set down at the right hand of the throne of God." Yes, a saint, a Christian, a Scriptural Christian is separated.

I had a dear friend in Oklahoma by the name of George Murray. He was seventy-some-odd years old when he died. He came from Georgia. You know, they have a lot of religion in that old State of Georgia. That man was one of the most religious Baptists I have ever known in my life. One night the singer and I had gone to bed in the home where we were staying during the revival, and "Uncle George" came walking into our room. We were sleeping in separate beds. He woke us up and said, "Boys, it is too late for me to go anywhere else. I wonder if you would mind doubling up and letting me sleep in one of your beds." The singer said he would be glad to, and he walked over and got into my bed. "Uncle George" sat down on his bed and took off his shoes and started to undress. Before he moved to get into the bed, he turned to us and said, "Boys, have you had prayer tonight?"

"Yes, we surely have."

"Would you mind praying with me again?"

"No, not at all," we said.

We got out of bed; got down on each side of that old man. He stretched out his great old arms and embraced us. The singer prayed. He prayed. Then I prayed. We went back to bed about eleven o'clock. That old man began to talk to us about what he had seen and heard. It was a blessing to hear it. When those old-time Christians get started, they surely can warm your heart. Some will not have much to tell when they get old. It is going to be a barren old age. Thank God, I have a geat deal to think about. I have much to praise God for. Anyway, "Uncle George" said, "Did you ever hear about the walking Christian?"

Fred said, "I have." Fred was the singer.

I said, "I haven't, Uncle George. I think Fred won't mind your telling me."

"All right, I'll tell you. Out yonder in Georgia where I came from, there was a little village at a cross-road. About a half mile along the right-hand road there was a little hill. The road went over the hill. Right there at that cross-road lived an old bachelor. He was the last one of his family. He didn't have any more kinsfolk left, and he was an atheist. He was an absolute infidel. In that village there lived a shoemaker.

Every Saturday morning about eleven o'clock that shoemaker would walk from the village store to the cross-
roads, turn to the right, walk past the infidel's house,
top the hill, cross over, disappear. Year after year,
every Saturday morning he would go out, and Monday
morning he would come back. The infidel watched the
man constantly, and greeted him once in a while. One
time he saw the shoemaker come along, take the right-
hand road, start up that hill, and continue out of sight.
Monday came, and the shoemaker didn't come back.
Tuesday, he didn't come back; Wednesday, he didn't
come back; Thursday, he didn't come back; Friday, he
didn't come back; Saturday, he didn't come back; and
the infidel couldn't stand it anymore. He drove to the
village and walked into the shoestore. A young woman
greeted him.

"Do you have a pair of shoes here?"

He said, "No."

"Do you want to leave a pair of shoes?"

"No. I want to see the man in charge."

"You mean my daddy?"

"I guess he is your daddy. I want to see the man in
charge of the store."

"Well, he is not here. He won't be back until next
Monday."

"Where is he?"

"You see it is like this. My daddy belongs to a
church of which there is no organization in this little
town. About two miles from the cross-roads on the
other side of the hill, there is another little town, and
there is a church there of our denomination. My daddy
goes out there to meeting. He goes out every Saturday
and comes back every Monday. He goes to service

Saturday night, Sunday morning, Sunday afternoon, and Sunday night."

"Where is he now?"

"They are having a revival there, and a great preacher has come there to preach. My daddy is too old to walk there every morning and come back every night, so some kinsfolk of ours asked him to come and stay for the two weeks and go to the meetings. That is where he is."

"Thank you, Sister," he said.

He walked out of that door and went home. All that afternoon he studied and mused over the matter. He couldn't understand it. He just couldn't understand it. He had been associating with Christians all his life, but he couldn't understand any man having that much religion. He got into his buggy and drove out to the village across the hill. When he got there, he asked the first man he met, "I have heard there is a revival in town. Where is it?"

"You go down past the post-office, turn the first block to the right, and go out to the edge of town. There in a meadow you will see a great big brush arbor, and that is where the meeting is."

By that time it was dark. He drove past the post-office, turned to the right, and came to the brush arbor where the services were being held. The people sang and prayed. The evangelist preached, gave the invitation, and the first man to come down the aisle to the mourner's bench was the infidel. Everybody knew him, knew his reputation, knew his age, knew he was an atheist. They began to weep and praise God. When the service was over, the preacher came up to him and asked, "Brother, we know you have been a hard case. We'd about given you up. Thank God, you are saved.

But tell me, what was there about my sermon that moved you?"

The man looked at him and said, "Brother, I don't suppose I could even tell you about what you preached."

The preacher looked as if somebody had dashed cold water in his face and said, "What was there about the singer's song that moved you?"

He said, "Well, as a matter of fact, I have heard better singers than he is many times."

"Well, what was there about the service?"

"Listen," he said, "if you will let me alone, I will tell you what it was. Do you see that old man right there, standing by that buggy? He is a shoemaker in my town, and for twenty-three years he has walked Christ."

That is what it takes. That is being a Scriptural Christian. Now, just close your eyes for a minute and think about how many you have in your town like that. How many walking Christians do you have in your town? Yes, sir. How many do you have? Oh, wait a minute, don't get excited. Don't think I am scolding you. I am not saying you have adulterers and murderers in your church. Don't misunderstand me. I don't mean that. I mean you have too many negative Christians. What we need is positive Christians, walking Christians.

Second, a Scriptural Christian is a soldier. Jesus said, "Let him take up his cross." A cross-bearing Christian is a soldier. I served in the United States army after the war. I was too young during the war. I was a staff sergeant in the Medical Department. I know what it takes to be a soldier. There are two things that make up a soldier, there are two things that make up a U. S. Army soldier, two things that make up a Christian soldier. A Scriptural Christian, a soldier, is one who is trained. He is trained. You say, "What application is there in that to Scriptural Christianity?"

I shall tell you. I believe every Christian who has been a Christian for any length of time ought to be able to pray in public. I believe that every Christian who has been a Christian for any length of time ought to be able to lead a prayer-meeting. I believe that every Christian who has been a Christian for any length of time ought to be able to teach a Sunday-school lesson. I believe a Christian who has been a Christian for any length of time ought to be able to tell a lost sinner out of the Bible what he has to do to be saved. I would hate to give most Christians an examination. I would hate to give the officers and leaders of this church an examination. Yet a Scriptural Christian should be trained in the Word of God. That is our weapon.

I remember when I came to the United States Army during the war. I was in college, in the Student's Army Training Corps. They gave me a rifle. I didn't know its parts. We were ordered to spread a blanket on the floor and take that rifle apart and put it together again, it seemed to me a hundred times. We would get our hands greasy and dirty taking it apart and putting it together again. But I became familiar enough with it so that after taking it apart in the dark I could put my hands on that bunch of metal, pick up this piece or that, and tell exactly what it was and where it belonged. I was trained. I believe a child of God ought to be trained that way in the Word of God and in the work of God.

Then a soldier, whether you are in the army of a nation or in the army of Christ, ought to be trustworthy, obedient, ready at any time by day or night

to serve his captain, to serve and obey his officers, to
go out at the drop of the hand to battle against the
enemy. Now, just think how little there is of that in
our churches. It is a heart-breaking fact. Think of the
Christ-crucifying fact, think of the soul-sending-to-hell
fact that even after two weeks of revival the average
church has not even awakened out of its sleep. After
the revival is over and scores of souls have been saved
and baptized into the membership of the church, the
majority of the members of the average church have not
even been aroused to their duty. Are they trustworthy?
Think of the fact that in a revival, which is a definite
battle of the hosts of God, of the army of God, against
the host and army of Satan, the commissioned and non-
commissioned officers, deacons, superintendents, teachers, young people's leaders, women's officials, have not
even put fingernail to fingernail together to help the
soldiers of the Lord to win the battle against the
soldiers of the devil. Isn't that generally tragically so?
It ought not to be.

I say Scriptural Christianity means that every
Christian-trained child of God, born again, washed
in the blood, is studying the Book and knows portions
of it by heart so that even when the Book is not available he can point an unsaved soul to the fact that he
is lost in sin and to the Lamb of God, Who stands ready
to take away his sin. I say again, every Scriptural
Christian has to be trustworthy. Are you trained? Are
you trustworthy? Ask the Holy Spirit to reveal your
condition to yourself.

Third, Scriptural Christianity is one more thing: a
Scriptural Christian is a savior. Not only is a Scriptural
Christian a saint, saved and separated; not only is a
Scriptural Christian a soldier, trained and trustworthy;

a Scriptural Christian is a savior. "Follow me, and I will make you fishers of men." Every Christian ought to be a savior. Now, you know what I mean. I don't mean that you and I can save souls, but let me give you an illustration.

I was in a revival in Denton, Texas. The Lord gave us a mighty victory. There were wonderful crowds, wonderful results. God was so blessedly good to us. The last night of the meeting came. The pastor had baptized. He had me stand in line to shake hands with the people as they walked out. After a while there came in that line a young student from T. C. W., the college for women. Her hair was still stringy wet from the baptistry. She took my hand in hers and, pumping it up and down, said, "Brother Appelman, I surely thank you for saving me."

I knew what she meant, and she knew that I knew what she meant. I didn't save her, but here is what happened. One night she raised her hand for prayer. I went back to her and plead with her, kneeling on the seat in front of her until she finally walked down the aisle and gave her heart to Christ. I had helped bring her to Christ. Do you see what I mean? Do you see what she meant?

Yes, every one of us ought to bring souls to Jesus— to be a savior.

To be saviors involves several essential qualifications. First, we must be purposeful. We must make up our minds that soul-winning is the work we are going to do; that fishing for men is the task God called us to; that it is our responsibility, our obligation, our duty. I sat in the pulpit of a church the second week of a revival as the singer asked how many had had prayers answered the day before. Not half of the people

present raised their hands. They hadn't prayed. The
singer asked how many were burdened for souls. Not
half their hands were raised, not half. They were not
burdened. They had no purpose. It is just that they
were Christians, saved, going to heaven—maybe. "Not
everyone who says heaven is going to get there." One
has to be a Scriptural Christian before he can get to
heaven. It has to be burned into one's heart, mind,
soul, and life before he gets to heaven. Some people
have an idea that faith means coming down the aisle
and saying, "I trust Christ to save me." The devil knows
more about Jesus than all of us put together, but he
is still the devil. Faith means taking yourself, lock,
stock, and barrel, and saying, "Jesus, here I am. Take
me over." Until you do that, you may shout and
screech and sing and sound all you please, but you
are a candidate for hell. You are not saved. There
must be a purpose—passionate, powerful, a Christ-like
purpose.

Do you want to be a soul-winner? Do you want to
be a savior? Do you want to have the privilege of
leading precious souls to Jesus Christ, the greatest
privilege God can give to men? Why, the angels in
heaven covet and envy the joy and opportunity of
telling the story of Christ and bringing men and women
and children to Jesus. Why, folks, the humblest Christian in this town who is a saint, a soldier, a savior,
who is trying to win the lost; the humblest Christian
in this town is doing more for God, more for Christ,
more for the world, than all the presidents, all the
kings, all the educators, all the legislators, all the
philosophers, all the philanthropists, this world has
ever seen put together. One immortal soul is worth

more than all the world beside. When you realize that, it gives you a purpose.

Second, a savior has to be not only purposeful but persistent. Soul-winning is an art. Saviorship is an art. You have to practice it to become proficient in it.

First, we must be persistent in right living. Our lives must be clean. God cannot use an unclean vessel. Our testimony will ring untrue unless our lives are clean. Sincerity of life, surrender of life, devotion of life, cleanness of life, beauty of life, are first requisites in this persistence in saviorhood.

Second, we must be persistent in loyalty to Christ. I don't believe a Christian who has not loved his Savior is going to win many souls to Christ, do you? I don't believe he will. He is not interested enough. His testimony is not true; his life just doesn't back up his testimony. He is just not going to do it. Loyalty to Christ engenders in our souls a fire, a compassion that God uses, a grappling-hook, as it were, in the hands of the Holy Ghost, to rescue these souls as brands from the burning.

He must be persistent in his loyalty to Christ, to the Bible, to the church. He must also be persistent in witness-bearing. You do not need me to tell that to you. You know that. Like any other art, the art of soul-winning becomes greater, more effective, more efficient, with practice. We must keep on keeping on, trying to win the lost to a saving acceptance of the Lord Jesus Christ. We must, before the revival, during the revival, after the revival, three hundred sixty-five days in the year, look for opportunities, make opportunities, use opportunities to tell the story of Christ and Him crucified. You will know that same joy of the harvest, the peace that "Uncle George" Murray was

talking about. You will be a walking Christian. I had
a preacher friend with me once, leading the singing in
a revival in south Texas. He came from Georgia.
The meeting was not going well. One day we were
praying, and I said, "Lord, if it is Your will, if it is
all right with You, let us close this meeting tonight
and go to the next place where they are waiting for
us. These people don't want a revival at all."

It didn't look as though they did. When I got through
praying, the singer reached into his pocket and pulled
out a post-card and said, "Look at this."

I read it. It said, "Tell that Jew boy that every
day your mother goes to Gethsemane and prays for
you two preacher boys."

I said, "What does she mean? Do they have a
place called Gethsemane up there?"

It was my first year in the ministry. I had been a
Christian five years, and I had studied my Bible very
little up to that time. I didn't get the Gethsemane
connection. He said, "No, we don't have a place up
there called Gethsemane."

"What did she mean then? Where does she go?"

"I will tell you," he said. "We live in a double farm-
house, with a corridor in the middle and rooms on both
sides. In back of the house, from the kitchen door to
milking barn, is a brick path. Back of the milking
barn is the barn lot. Beyond that is the cotton patch.
A little farther is a stand of timber. My mother goes
out to that stand of timber and prays. She calls it her
Gethsemane."

I understood it then.

"When does she go there? How long does she
stay? Does she go there every day? Does she go
alone?"

He said, "I will tell you all about it if you will not interrupt." He said, "Listen, my mother goes out there all alone. She never takes anybody with her."

"How often does she go?" I asked.

"She goes out there every day. Hyman, I have seen my mother put on Dad's hip-boots and rubber slicker and go out in the driving snow or rain and pray. She goes there right after dinner. Sometimes it is thirty minutes, sometimes an hour, sometimes it is dark, and we are doing the chores when she comes back. Sometimes she comes back smiling. Sometimes she comes back crying. Sometimes she comes back singing. Sometimes she is patting her hands. Sometimes she is walking slowly. Sometimes she is walking fast."

I said, "Do you mean she goes out there every day of the year?"

He said, "Listen, a tree fell and crippled my Daddy. He spent fourteen months in bed. Every day my mother would call in one of the children to sit by that bed while she would go out to her Gethsemane and pray."

"Let me pray again. I want to add a postscript to my prayer. I would like to change it." I said, "Lord, I have changed my mind. Forget what I have just said. Lord, You use us two preachers to answer that Georgia woman's prayer."

He did. He broke that community apart for Christ. It is all different now. There is a good church out there with regular services.

The years went past. In 1936, I was at the Navarro County Association meeting. Another preacher friend, one of the singer's and my prayer partners, came up to me and said, "Hyman, I have been to see Fred's mother."

"Tell me about her."

"Let's sit down here between these automobiles where we can't be seen."

"Tell me what she looks like."

He said, "Fred and I and Ellen (that's Fred's wife) and David (that's Fred's boy) went to Atlanta. We stopped at his home. His mother was expecting us. We shook hands, talked for awhile, then she went into the kitchen to get dinner ready. I walked around that place. I looked at the chickens and the pigs. I looked at the barns. I came back into the house and walked into the kitchen again. I thought I would go in there and see the lady. She told me to get out, that she was too busy to 'mess around' with any preachers. I went around that house, and I went into a room. It seemed like a kind of parlor. There was an old-time organ. There was some old-time music on a stand. It made me homesick for my own **Mamma**." He said he walked across the hall into the bedrooms. There were four of them in a row, the last one looking out toward the fields. It must have been the mother's room, he said, because it had an old-time four-post bed in it. Did you ever see one of them—the kind with a roof on it? It had curtains tied to the posts. Did you ever see one? I was born in one in Russia. Right by the side of that bed was an old-time, round table with a great big slab of blue-veined marble on it. Did you ever see one of those tables with a fat slab of marble on top as a cover? It had one leg underneath that spread out like lions' claws on the bottom. On the top of the table was an old kerosene lamp with a chimney and a wick. By the side of that lamp on that table was a Bible, a Georgia Baptist magazine, a teacher's quarterly.

He said, "It broke my heart. I got down on my knees by the side of that bed, bowed my head on that bed, and wept my heart out in prayer. After awhile the call came for supper. About six o'clock we sat down, fifteen of us. We ate and ate and ate and ate. It was the best Georgia dinner I had ever eaten in my life. It got to be around eight o'clock. One of the boys stood up and lit the kerosene lamp on the mantel. There was no electricity out there. After awhile the mother turned to me and said, "Brother Nelson, I know you are from the city.' She didn't know I was just a country preacher. But if she wanted to think I was a 'city slicker,' I didn't care. 'Now, you know, we go to bed early here. If you want to stay up, that is all right, but I am going to bed on time. Before we go to bed, let's all move our chairs to the fireplace and have our evening prayer-meeting.' The fireplace, of course, didn't have any fire in it. It was in July.

"The mother sat down in a great big arm-chair with her children and grandchildren around her. She lifted up her hand toward the mantelpiece and, without looking (she knew right where it was) brought down her Bible. She reached up her hand and didn't even look. She just got hold of that old Bible and pulled it down onto her knees and began to look around for something. She looked in her pocket, she looked in the Bible, and passed her hand over the mantelpiece, searching for something. After awhile, one little grandchild in a kind of disgusted voice said, 'Grandma, they are on your forehead.'

"Grandma pulled her glasses down. She grinned a bit, fitted them on, and opened her Bible to one of the Psalms, and in that soft, gentle, sweet, warm Georgia voice, she read some Scripture. Then she said, 'Children, the Lord understands. I am too old and too heavy to kneel. I will sit here, and the rest of you kneel around and pray. Brother Nelson, you begin, and I will close.' "

He said, "I prayed. The next one prayed. The little children prayed. Everyone of them said about the same thing as if they had memorized it. It got to be the mother's turn. The room got quiet, very quiet. She didn't say anything for a long while. After some minutes, we began to hear her hands pass across the Bible, loving it and petting it."

Have you ever done that? I have. I have come to the end of my row a great many times. I've said to God, "Lord, I am doing the best I know how. If I am doing wrong, straighten me out." And I have gotten peace out of this old Book. I always get it. It has never failed me yet.

After a while, he said, the mother began to pray. It seemed that the ceiling spread open and the starry night disappeared. Heaven itself opened wide as God bent down from glory to catch the whispered syllables of that old saint.

The story-teller put his arm around me, drew me to himself, and said, "Hyman, that widow raised a family of six children. Five of them went to college. One was sacrificed. The oldest one had to stay at home and work. She has taught a Sunday-school class in that one-room church at her home for years. During the forty-some-odd years she has taught that Sunday-school class, sixty-three young men and young women have gone out of her class to become denominational leaders in the Southern Baptist Convention.

Think of it! a Georgia town with not three hundred people at any time there, a widow, a saint, a soldier, a savior, and her influence reaching out and out until it touches God, heaven, eternity. See what you and I could do with our advantages. With our added opportunities; with our greater openings; with our wider responsibilities; consequently privileges, how much more ought we to do for Christ.

God give each of us the grace to make a greater impact on the world by living out our Scriptural Christianity for the glory of Jesus. Amen.

VII

BLOOD PURGE

This then is the message which we have heard of him, and declare unto you, that God is light, and in him is no darkness at all. If we say that we have fellowship with him, and walk in darkness, we lie, and do not the truth: But if we walk in the light, as he is in the light, we have fellowship one with another, and the blood of Jesus Christ his Son cleanseth us from all sin. If we say that we have no sin, we deceive ourselves, and the truth is not in us. If we confess our sins, he is faithful and just to forgive us our sins, and to cleanse us from all unrighteousness. If we say that we have not sinned, we make him a liar, and his word is not in us. My little children, these things write I unto you, that ye sin not. And if any man sin, we have an advocate with the Father, Jesus Christ the righteous. And he is the propitiation for our sins: and not for ours only, but also for the sins of the whole world.
— I JOHN 1:5 - 2:2

I AM taking this entire passage as my text,—stressing especially that statement: "The bood of Jesus Christ his Son cleanseth us from all sin." This verse unquestionably is the key verse to the entire Bible. Someone has said that the second coming of Christ is the key to Scripture. Now, I don't know whether that is so or not; but I do know that in the message of the blood of Jesus is the unfolding of God's Word. I believe that the whole Bible is written for one purpose,

100

and that is to tell us that nineteen hundred years ago Jesus Christ died on the cross and that in His blood any man and every man, any woman and every woman, any child and every child, may have the remission, the forgiveness, the free pardon of sin.

This message is very dear, very cheering, very inspiring to me, first of all, because it says, "The blood of Jesus Christ," not the blood of some man, not the blood of some animal, not the blood to be spilled in a certain fashion upon a given altar, but the blood of Jesus Christ that has already been poured out on Calvary.

The second reason this message means so much to me is because it does not say the blood of Jesus Christ, His Son, *cleansed* or *will cleanse; it says cleanses.* That means it cleanses now. It means it cleanses tomorrow. It means it cleanses the next day. It means it cleanses the day after. It means it keeps on cleansing for so long as this poor sinner needs cleansing and, for that matter, in the selfsame fashion, for so long as any other sinner in the world needs that cleansing, coursing tide. I wish I had time to develop this thought. You know this word was written originally in Greek, and in the Greek that word "cleanses" means "continues to cleanse, without hesitation, without stopping."

A man will come to us and say, "Suppose you are converted and then go out and sin?" Well, the answer is, "The blood of Jesus Christ, his Son, cleanses us from all sin."

"But suppose a man is converted and goes out and kills somebody?" The answer still is, "The blood of Jesus Christ, his Son, cleanses us from all sin."

"Suppose a man goes out after he is converted and leaves the church and never comes back, and so on, and on, and on, and on, until the day he dies?" "The blood of Jesus Christ, his Son, cleanses us from all sin." It says "all sin"—any kind, every kind, all kinds of sin.

That is a mighty declaration to us who are Christians. It gives us hope, confidence, assurance. It gives us a weapon against besetting sin and temptation. It gives us an instrument of warfare against the devil and all of his traps and tricks. Surely it is the most hopeful passage in the entire Bible to the unsaved soul. The fact that back yonder, nineteen hundred years ago, on Calvary's cross, God opened the veins of His Son and poured out His Son's blood unto death is a guarantee written in the blood of God's Son, punctuated by the agony of that Son on Calvary, that God has saved, that God does save, and that God will save all those who come unto Him by way of the cross, by way of the Christ, by way of the shed blood.

But nobody will come to Jesus to ask for that blood unless he realizes the need of it. So let us take this verse, this text, apart. Let us think of it for awhile along these three lines. First, the fact of sin, the need for this blood; second, the provision of that blood; third, the application of that blood, what must we do in order to receive, in order to be washed in that cleansing blood.

1. THE FACT OF SIN

Sin is the universal difficulty of man and of God. It is in every home; it is in every heart; it is in every life. Any way you analyze it, any way you study it, balance it, read of it, observe it, experience it, it does three things to us. Everything else that sin does will fit into one of these three pigeon-holes.

The first thing that sin does is that it estranges man
from God and God from man. It puts a barrier between God and man. It puts a crevice, a river, an im-
passable ocean between God and man that God cannot
cross to reach man and man cannot cross to reach God.
There is nothing else in the life of a mortal soul that
can drive God out. You can be rich and have all of
God. You can be poor and have all the fulness of
God's presence and God's power in your life. You
can be educated and be just as godly as you please.
You can be ignorant and have an abundance of spiritual knowledge that will make you walk with the princes
of God's realm and not be ashamed of rubbing shoulders with them. You can be a Jew or a Gentile, a
man, a woman, a child, young or old, weak or strong;
it makes not a particle of difference. One thing, just
one thing, can drive God from our lives, and that is
sin. Sin undoubtedly, unquestionably, indubitably, universally, everlastingly separates between God and man
in life, in death, in the judgment, throughout an eternity, as the soul of the sinner is plunged, banished from
the presence of God, into the bottomless pit of everlasting torment where there is nothing of God to be
seen, experienced, or known.

The second thing that sin does is that it enslaves
man—enslaves his appetites, his ambitions, his thoughts,
his affections, his conscience. Everything there is about
man that the devil can tie up in the chains of sin, the
devil enslaves. Listen, I read somewhere of an incident
that will better illustrate what I am trying to tell you
than anything I can say.

A French captain was walking along the shore at
Dover, England, just walking along and looking out
to sea, when suddenly he stumbled and fell to one

knee. He noticed that his right foot had caught in the link of a chain, a great cable, an anchor chain rusted with the abandoned years. He started to pull his foot out and it wouldn't come out. He twisted it and turned it and kept on turning and twisting it. He was a strong man, and the first thing he knew the foot began to swell. He untied his shoe, thinking he would pull out his stockinged foot, kept on pulling and straining, tried to lift the cable, but to no avail. It was embedded in the sand! The cold chills crept up his body. The tide was beginning to wash across his feet. He was frightened. He knew he had to get out of there quickly. He waited for the water to cover his foot, thinking it would cool off and get a little smaller, but it wouldn't work. The tide kept on coming in. It was almost up to his knees. There were some men fishing off shore. He called to them, but before he made them understand, the tide had gone above his knees. He had been there for over an hour. The tide kept on coming in. The men came to him. He told them his predicament. They tried to lift the cable but could not budge it. The tide kept on creeping up. One of the men waded to the shore, ran to the village and brought a blacksmith with a saw to cut the cable. The blacksmith had to work in the water. Something happened, and the saw snapped. There was just one more thing to do! The man made for the village again to bring the doctor. By the time he got back, the water was more than waist high. The village doctor tried to cut off that man's limb, but he couldn't work in the water. Those poor people had to stand by and see that French captain drown. He was enslaved by that cable.

Listen! I wish I had time to tell you story after story of the many times some of us preachers have had to stand by and see men's souls drown in sin. It is a tragic truth. What are we preachers going to do? Any pastor or preacher who stays in a community long enough sees the sea of sin swallow up many souls enslaved, entrapped in sin. You play around with the devil, go on rejecting Christ, resisting the Spirit, saying "no" to the gospel, and one of these days you will not be able to pull your foot out. You will just work and toil while the chain of sin drags you out of life down into hell.

The third thing sin does is that it inescapably, inevitably, universally, unqualifiedly, unchangeably entails death. Not only does it estrange man from God, not only does it enslave man, but it entails death. "The wages of sin is death." It is death to character, death to reputation, death to love, death to ambition, death to influence, death to chances of getting ahead in the world, death to the mind, death to the heart, death to the body, and finally death to the soul, which we call "the second death."

Surely that poet was more than justified when he wrote:

There is not one evil that sin has not brought me,
There is not one good that has come in its train;
It has cursed me through life, and its sorrows have
sought me
Every step of the way through want, sickness and
pain.
And then, when this life of affliction is ended,
Oh! what a home for my weary soul did it
prepare!
The wrath of Him whom my sins have offended,
And the night, the dark night of eternal despair.

God, help you to see it! Those three things are inescapable. There is no way out of them except through Christ. Sin estranges from God. Sin enslaves man, the best man, the cleanest man, the biggest man, the strongest man. Sin enslaves the heart, the mind, the will. Sin irrevocably entails death.

There are some people who are so fooled and so eagerly fooling themselves that they think they need no salvation. They think they are all right. They compare themselves with the wicked people around them. Their lives are cleaner than the lives of those who are in gross sin. They say, "I don't need the blood of Jesus." They compare themselves with the backslidden condition of some church-members, and say: "I am as good as they are." Consequently they think they can get to heaven, not on their own merit but on the demerit of others. Did you ever hear anything so silly in your life as to expect to get to heaven on the faults of other people? Because the church-members are hypocrites, they expect to go to heaven. I never heard a Jew say that. It takes a Gentile to say that. He doesn't try to go on the other man's mistakes, on the other man's failures and shortcomings, but a great many people do. "If we say we have no sin the truth is not in us. If we say we have not sinned, we make him a liar, and his word is not in us."

There are some people who think they can cure themselves. There are some people who think they can give up drinking, gambling, give up adultery, give up cursing, give up this sin, that sin, the other sin, and by letting go of some overt sins get to heaven that way. No, beloved, you can't do it. Jesus told a parable of how a demon was driven out of a man. The man didn't do a thing further about it, didn't surrender his will to the Lord, didn't follow Him in baptism, in church-membership, in service. The demon went around in divers places looking for a home. He came back and found that man in the selfsame position he was in before. Calling a half-dozen other demons he came into that man's heart, life, mind, and the man was worse after the expulsion than he was before it happened.

No, you can't pull yourself up by your bootstraps. You can't do it. The law of gravity, spiritual as well as natural, will not permit you to do it. You can't lift yourself out of sin into goodness, into salvation. You can't lift yourself out of hell. You can't lift yourself into heaven. You are not wise enough, not strong enough, not courageous enough, not big enough. You don't even have control of your own thoughts, let alone of your own emotions.

Some people depend on other things besides the blood to cure them. There are many who depend on their having been sprinkled into the church when children. I have had people tell me, "Why, sure, I am a Christian. I don't remember the time when I wasn't a Christian." That statement in itself proves they never have been saved. Why, every child of God remembers the day—I don't mean the exact day of the week or month—I mean the experience, when he gave his heart to Christ. If you have never had an experience like that, you have never been saved. You say, "What are you trying to do—make us all have the same experience?" No. I am trying to tell you that you do have an experience with God when you are converted. You know it. That is what we mean when we say "heartfelt religion." You know it. God does something to your heart, does something to your soul, to your life. With some of us who were very bad the transformation

was more striking than it is with others, but every one
of us will have a transformation. No, you can't depend
on the fact that you were immersed nor on the fact that
you were sprinkled as a child into the church.

There is only one answer to man's sin. God's answer
is, "The blood of Jesus Christ, his Son, cleanses us
from all sin." If there were any other way, if God
could forgive us in any other way, cleanse us from unrighteousness in any other way, save us from hell in
any other way, take us to heaven in any other way,
Jesus would never have died on the cross. The blood,
and the blood alone, can cleanse us, can save us, can
keep us from our sins.

Why is that? Because the Bible says so. Where does
it say so? Listen! I told you in the beginning of my
sermon sin does three things: first, it estranges God;
second, it enslaves man; third, it entails death. Now,
the blood of Jesus Christ answers these three problems.

2. The Provision of the Blood

The blood of Jesus Christ, God's Son, reconciles us
to God. We are no longer estranged from God. We are
no longer enemies of God, no longer aliens to the commonwealth of Israel, no longer in open rebellion against
the holy law. It is written: "God was in Christ reconciling the world unto himself, not imputing their trespasses unto them." Again it is written, "But God com-
mendeth his love toward us, in that, while we were
yet sinners, Christ died for us. Much more, then, being
now justified by his blood, we shall be saved from
wrath through him. For if when we were enemies we
were reconciled to God by the death of his Son, much
more being reconciled we shall be saved by his life."

Again it is written, "And having made peace through

the blood of his cross by him to reconcile all things unto himself." This is the first thing the blood does. It breaks down the barrier. It bridges the chasm, so we can come to God and God can come to us. Beloved, that is so on the authority of God's Word. Take it and rejoice in it. Take it, receive it, and live by it. That is so. God says so. We are reconciled to God by the blood of His only begotton Son, so that we are no longer enemies but children, subjects of God almighty, citizens of heaven.

The second thing I told you was that sin enslaved man, sold him to the Law, to his own appetites, sold him to the judgments and the justice of God. Along comes the blood of Jesus and redeems us from the slavery of sin. It is written, "Christ hath redeemed us from the curse of the law, being made a curse for us: for it is written, Cursed is every one which hangeth on a tree." Jesus Christ hung on a tree, on Calvary's tree. God made Him a curse for us, and by His blood He redeemed us from the curse of the Law. Again it is written, "In whom we have redemption, the forgiveness of our sins, through faith in his blood." The blood provides for redemption. Again it is written, "Forasmuch as ye know that ye were not redeemed with corruptible things, such as silver and gold, from your sins, but with the precious blood of Christ as of a lamb without blemish and without spot." Beloved, just step out on the promises that I have given you. Don't hesitate; don't be afraid; don't look at your own sins. I know, God knows, you know, you have plenty of them. We all have. Look to Jesus; look to Calvary; look to the blood. Remember that Christ paid for your redemption. If you will come to God, regardless of who or what you are, God will give you a bill paid in full and receipted in the blood of His Son. Thank God for that! I told you further that sin entails death, that sin kills. The blood of Jesus Christ makes alive. The blood of Christ not only reconciles, not only redeems, but it regenerates. Listen! "For we ourselves also were sometimes foolish, disobedient, deceived, serving divers lusts and pleasures, living in malice and envy, hateful, and hating one another. But after that the kindness and love of God our Savior toward men appeared, not by works of righteousness which we have done, but according to his mercy he saved us, by the washing of regeneration, and renewing of the Holy Ghost; which he shed on us abundantly through Jesus Christ our Savior." It is the blood of Jesus Christ that regenerates the soul, the blood of Jesus Christ that purchases life for us. Don't forget that. It is written, "He that believeth on the Son hath everlasting life." He that believeth on the Son has life because the Son bought that life; because the Son paid for that life; because the Son passed that life on to us. I will take time to give you an illustration that I know you will not forget in a hurry.

During our Civil War, William Scott, a soldier in the Union army, fell asleep at Key Bridge. He was found asleep, tried by court-martial, and sentenced to die. His mother came to the President, Abraham Lincoln, begging, pleading for his release. Finally Abe said, "All right, I will let him go." He took a carriage, drove to the guard-house, and walked in. The boy looked up, recognized him, and saluted. The President sat down. The boy stood in front of him. "William, did you fall asleep? Do you know what might have happened if the enemy had marched over and killed hundreds of our boys? Did you get a fair trial? Do you deserve to die?" The great, hot tears coursed down the boy's cheeks. "Yes, Mr. President," he said, "I am guilty and deserve to die." "William," said the President, "I am going to let you go; but, remember, your life belongs to me." William went back to his ranks, to his company. The war went on. Came Gettysburg, that fearful battle. William was charging with the Union troops when a Confederate bullet found his body, wounding him mortally. His friend stopped, turned back, raised his head. William said, "John, there is nothing you can do for me. I will be dead in a minute. He reached down into his blouse and pulled out some trinkets. "I want you to give these to my mother. Tell her how I died." Drawing a deep breath, he said, "Bud, listen! When this war is over they are going to take you soldiers and march you through Washington in the victory march. I want you, if you get a chance to fall out of the ranks, to go to the White House, look up Abraham Lincoln, and tell him William Scott gave him back his life on Gettysburg battlefield."

You know what that boy meant. We were all sentenced. We had a fair trial. We deserved to die. God didn't come down and sit down in our bunks and stand us in front of Him and say, "I am going to let you go." He did more than that. He sent His Son to Calvary to take our place. God is offering life and freedom, salvation and power, to every soul because of what His Son did on Calvary's cross. There you have it. Sin estranges from God: the blood reconciles to God. Sin enslaves man: the blood redeems man. Sin entails death: the blood gives you new life.

3. The Application, the Way of Receiving the Blood

We have but one more question, one more word, one more statement. What must we do? What must any of us do to avail ourselves of that blood? Let God tell you. "If we walk in the light as he is in the light, we have fellowship one with another, and the blood of Jesus Christ his Son cleanseth us from all sin." Walk in the light. That is the answer. What does it mean to walk in the light? It means to walk in the light of God's Word. It means to do what God tells you to do in His Word. What does it mean to do what God tells us to do? It means three things.

God said through His Son, "Except ye repent, ye shall all likewise perish." "Except ye be converted and become as a little child, ye shall in no wise enter the kingdom of heaven." John says, "If we confess our sins he is faithful and just to forgive us our sins and to cleanse us from all unrighteousness." Repentance is the willingness, the anxiety to give up our sins. I used to think that repentance meant to give up your sins. Preachers preach that way and commentators write that way. Of all men I was the most miserable, because I knew I could not in my own strength give up my sins. Then when I began to study and analyze the Word, I found that what God says is, "Here is my hand; you take hold of it and I will pull you out of the pit, put your feet on the rock, send you on your way rejoicing." Repentance means being sorry enough, concerned enough, anxious enough, worried enough, burdened enough about the sins that are taking you to hell to cry to God for help to lift you out of those sins. Repentance is a willingness, an eagerness, an anxiety to give up your sinful ways if God will give you the grace to do it.

The second thing is this: Where shall I start? A hundred Scriptures come to my mind. Listen! "God so loved the world that he gave his only begotten Son that whosoever believeth on him shall not perish but have everlasting life." "Verily, I say unto you, he that heareth my word, and believeth on him that sent me, hath everlasting life, and shall not come into condemnation; but is passed from death unto life." "Being justified freely by his grace, through the redemption which is in Christ Jesus; whom God hath set forth to be a propitiation through faith in his blood, to declare his righteousness for the remission of sins that are past." "In whom we have redemption, the forgiveness of our sins, through faith in his blood." "He that believeth is not condemned." "He that believeth hath life." "Believe on the Lord Jesus Christ, and thou shalt be saved." Over and over again God tells us that the second step toward Christ is faith, faith in Jesus, faith in His love, faith in His death, faith in His resurrection, faith in His mighty power, faith in His willingness, His ability to forgive our sins.

The third step in the light is this: If we walk in the light of repentance, in the light of faith, then, beloved, we must also follow on in the light of confession. Jesus Christ said, "Whosoever shall confess me before men him will I also confess before my Father in heaven." Jesus said through Paul, "If thou shalt confess with thy mouth the Lord Jesus and shalt believe in thine heart that God hath raised him from the dead, thou shalt be saved." God wants you to be willing to give up your sins, to embrace Christ as your Savior, to step out and confess Him honorably, honestly, loyally,

lovingly, openly before men. God promises that He
will wash away your sins, blot out your transgressions,
cover your iniquities, save you from death unto life,
keep you from hell, and take you to heaven.

The way is as open as the arms of Christ stretched
out on the cross. Every man, every woman, every child
may come and avail himself or herself of that shed
blood and be forever saved, forever a child of God,
forever a citizen and a subject of glory.

It was Charles G. Finney who told this story. He
was holding a revival in Detroit. One night as he
started to walk into the church, a man came up to him.
"Are you Dr. Finney?"

"Yes."

"I wonder if you will do me a favor. When you
get through tonight, will you come home with me and
talk to me about my soul?"

"Gladly. You wait for me." Finney walked inside,
and some of the men stopped him.

"What did the man want, Brother Finney?"

"He wanted me to go home with him."

"Don't do it."

"I am sorry, but I promised and I shall go with him."

When the service was over, Finney started out the
door. The man was waiting, took his arm, and said,
"Come with me." They walked three or four blocks,
turned into a side street, walked down an alley, and
at the second house the man stopped. "Stay here a
minute, Brother Finney." He reached into his pocket,
pulled out a key, unlocked the door, turned to the
preacher and said, "Come in." Mr. Finney walked into
the room. There was a carpet on the floor, a mantelpiece, a desk, a swivel chair, two arm chairs. There
was nothing else. There was a kind of a thin board

partition all round the room except where the fireplace was. Finney turned around. The man had locked the door, had reached into his back pocket, had pulled out a revolver, and was holding it in his hand. "I don't intend to do you any harm," he said. "I just want to ask you some questions. Did you mean what you said in your sermon last night?"

"What did I say? I have forgotten."

"You said, 'The blood of Jesus Christ cleanses us from all sin.'"

Finney said, "Yes, God says so."

The man said, "Brother Finney, you see this revolver? It has killed four people. It is mine. Two of them were killed by me, two of them by my bartender in a brawl in my saloon. Is there hope for a man like me?"

Finney said, "The blood of Jesus Christ cleanseth us from all sin."

The man said, "Brother Finney, another question. In back of this partition is a saloon. I own it, everything in it. We sell every kind of liquor to anybody who comes along. Many, many times I have taken the last penny out of a man's pocket, letting his wife and children go hungry. Many times women have brought their babies here and plead with me not to sell any more booze to their husbands, but I have driven them out and kept right on with the whiskey selling. Is there hope for a man like me?"

Finney said, "God says, 'The blood of Jesus Christ his Son cleanseth us from all sin.'"

"Another question, Brother Finney. In back of this other partition is a gambling joint, and it is as crooked as sin, as crooked as Satan. There isn't a decent wheel in the whole place. It is all loaded and crooked. A man leaves the saloon with some money left ir his pocket, and we take his money away from him in there. Men have gone out of that gambling place to commit suicide when their money and perhaps entrusted funds were all gone. Is there any hope for a man like me?"

Finney said, "God says, 'The blood of Jesus Christ his Son cleanseth us from all sin.' "

"One more question, and I will let you go. When you walk out of this alley, you turn to the right toward the street, look across the street, and there you will see a two-story brown stone house. It is my home. I own it. My wife is there, and my eleven-year-old child, Margaret. Thirteen years ago I went to New York on business. I met a beautiful girl. I lied to her. I told her I was a stock broker, and she married me. I brought her here, and when she found out my business it broke her heart. I have made life a hell on earth for her. I have come home drunk, beaten her, abused her, locked her out, made her life more miserable than that of any brute beast. About a month ago I went home one night drunk, mean, miserable. My wife got in the way somehow, and I started beating her. My daughter threw herself between us. I slapped that girl across the face and knocked her against a red-hot stove. Her arm is burned from shoulder to wrist. It will never look like anything decent. Brother Finney, is there hope for a man like me?"

Finney got hold of that man's shoulders, shook him, and said: "O son, what a black story you have to tell! But God says, 'The blood of Jesus Christ his son cleanseth us from all sin.' "

The man said, "Thank you. Thank you very much. Pray for me. I am coming to church tomorrow night."

Finney went about his business. The next morning, about seven o'clock, the saloon man started across the

street out of his office. His necktie was awry. His face
was dusty and sweaty and tear-stained. He was shaking
and rocking as though he were drunk. But let us go
back to that room. He had taken that swivel chair and
smashed the mirror, the fireplace, the desk, and the
other chairs. He had smashed the partition on each
side. Every bottle and barrel and bar and mirror in
that saloon was shattered and broken up. The sawdust
was swimming ankle-deep in a terrible mixture of
beer, gin, whiskey, and wine. In the gambling establish-
ment, the tables were smashed, the dice and cards
were in the fireplace smoldering. He staggered across
the street, walked up the stairs of his home, and sat
down heavily in the chair in his room. His wife called
the little girl, "Maggie, run upstairs and tell Daddy
breakfast is ready." The girl walked slowly up the
stairs. Half afraid, she stood in the door and said,
"Daddy, Mamma said breakfast was ready; to come
down."

"Maggie, darling, Daddy doesn't want any breakfast."

That little girl didn't walk; she just flew down the
stairs. "Mamma, Daddy said, 'Maggie, darling,' and
he didn't—"

"Maggie, you didn't understand. You go back upstairs and tell Daddy to come down." Maggie went
back upstairs with the mother following her. The man
looked up as he heard the child's step, spread his
knees out, and said, "Maggie, come here."

Shyly, frightened, in a tremble, the little girl walked
up to him. He lifted her, put her on his knee, pressed
his face against her breast, and wept. The wife, standing in the door, didn't know what had happened. After
awhile he noticed her and said, "Wife, come here."

He sat her down on his other knee, threw his big man's arms around those two whom he loved, whom he had so fearfully abused, lowered his face between them, and sobbed until the room almost shook with the impact of his emotion.

After some minutes, he controlled himself, looked up into the faces of his wife and girl, and said: "Wife, daughter, you needn't be afraid of me anymore. God has brought you a new man, a new Daddy, home today."

That same night that man, his wife, their child, walked down the aisle of the church, gave their hearts to Christ, and joined the church. He became an elder. Finney wrote that story in a sermon. I read it and am passing it on to you.

Thank God, "the blood of Jesus Christ his Son cleanseth us from all sin." Just come and accept that cleansing blood from the hands of God. Will you do it? Why should you wait? Why should you tarry? Why should you stain your soul, waste your life, break the heart of God and Christ, break your own heart, break the hearts of your loved ones, when you can come and be sure, certain, for time and for eternity, that your sins are cleansed and washed away in the blood of Christ?

Beloved, God will apply the blood of His Son to your soul. May God, in His grace, for Jesus' sake, help you.   Amen.

VIII

THE PRICE OF SOULS

Who hath heard such a thing? who hath seen such things? Shall the earth be made to bring forth in one day? or shall a nation be born at once? for as soon as Zion travailed, she brought forth her children.
—Isa. 66:8

ORIGINALLY the name Zion denoted the mount on which Solomon's Temple stood. In later years, the whole city of Jerusalem was called Zion. Still later all of Palestine came to be known as Zion. Still later all of the Jews, scattered to the ends of the earth, as a nation, in prophetic and rabbinic writings, came under the term "Zion." Today the church, the church of the living God, the body of the blessed Christ, all born-again, blood-washed, spirit-regenerated children of God, all of the souls that can truthfully and Scripturally lay claim to salvation, are Zion. Travail is a term that is familiar to all of us. Perhaps there is no agony that is comparable with the pain suffered by a woman in child-birth. The prophet adds these terms in the terrific statement of the text, "For as soon as Zion travailed she brought forth her children." The implication is clear. When the people of God become so burdened for the souls of sinners about them that they

119

suffer agony and anguish, that they are willing to make
a highway of their lives to the cross of Calvary, when
they spend nights of passionate intercession and days
of vigilant toil, Zion will bring forth her children.
The shouts of newborn souls will be heard in the
corridors of glory. That is as it should be.

Travail is the secret of the success in this workaday
world, in every sphere of human activity. Great lawyers are not made overnight, neither are great doctors,
nor are great engineers. Greatness, success, victory
in any pursuit, must be paid for by toil, by effort, by
self-denial, by unremitting pursuit. The price of achieve-
ment comes very high. Consider the travail of a mother
rearing one or more children. Think of the sleepless
nights, of the drivingly busy days; think of the agony
of wearying hours of nursing the sick little ones. What
real mother does not pay the full price of travail for
the children of her heart?

Travail built the church. The world criticizes us
because of the blood theology we proclaim. They say
there is too much blood in our religion. That is not
so. There is not enough blood. When we cease bleeding, we cease blessing. There is not enough sacrificial
blood spilled by the present Christian generation. The
blood of Jesus, the travailing, agonizing, torment-drawn
blood of Jesus laid the foundations of the church. Its
walls were erected and cemented together with the sacrificed bodies and spilled blood of the martyrs that have
trodden the holy road of Calvary in the footsteps of the
Master. Blood, blood, oceans of blood, blood of men,
of women, of children, streaming oceans wide across
the pages of Christian history, has marked the progress
of the church. Blood wrote the New Testament. Blood
sealed the testimony of first-century Christianity. Blood

brought in the Reformation. Blood laid the foundation
for missions. Blood preserved the faith of our fathers
in the dark centuries of Romish night. Blood spanned
the seas, bridged the rivers, crossed the continents,
tunneled the mountains, heralded the words of life to
the nations and the kingdoms and the tribes of the
earth. Yes, by the agony of Calvary, by the torment
of the martyred dead, by the crucified Peter, by the
beheaded Paul, by the blood-soaked Roman arenas, by
the dungeoned victims of the Inquisition, by the bones
of Huntington, by the enshrined heart of Livingstone,
by the Bedford Jail of Bunyan, by the loneliness of
Roger Williams, by the snow-melting prayer-sweat of
David Brainerd, by the torn wrists and wounded, bleeding ankles of Ava's Judson, by the Siberian-exiled
Russian Christians, by the concentration-camped German
Niemöller, travail built the church.

The greatest need of today, in the church and outside
of it, is travailing Christians. We have educated, talented, wealthy, socially active, politically successful,
world-admired, high-positioned Christians. We have
Christian doctors of world repute, Christian lawyers of
international importance, Christian bankers, statesmen,
generals, educators, scientists, that sway the destiny of
the earth. Our need is travailing Christians, weeping
Christians, sacrificial Christians. Christianity is not
a name but a need, not a title but a task, not a condition
but a challenge, a challenge to the loftiest, the holiest,
the noblest, the purest in us and among us. Christianity
is a heroic undertaking to mold a world in every detail
of its activities. Christianity is a religion for and of
heroes and heroines. "It does not take much of a man
to be a Christian, but it takes all there is of him."
Dry-eyed, sober-sided, passionless, emotionless Chris-

tianity will not save a world. It will take blood earnest-
ness, sleepless nights, compassion-driven days. We need
weeping Christians.

In the South some years ago one of our really great
evangelists held a revival. The Lord's blessings were
upon it. The crowds came. Scores were saved and
added to the church. One evening, a young-appearing
mother came to speak to the preacher.

"Brother Evangelist," she said, "I should like to ask
you a very vital question. I have three children—a girl
six years old, a boy of twelve, and another boy of fifteen. The little girl is perhaps too young to understand,
but the boys are old enough to be saved. I've tried to
talk to them about Christ and their souls, but they will
not listen to me. They come to church all right, but
they seemingly are absolutely untouched. Tell me, what
can I do with them?"

The evangelist studied the woman a moment.
"Madam," he said, "may I ask you some questions?
I presume you are a Christian. Is your husband?"

"Yes, sir, and one of the choicest souls I know. He
is a deacon and teaches a Sunday-school class."

"Do you have a family altar in your home? Do you
have grace over meat?"

"Indeed we do, sir. We have family worship twice
each day and grace at every meal."

"Do you go to church services consistently and take
your children with you?"

"Brother preacher, I guess that perhaps our entire
family are the most consistent attendants of the church
services of anybody in the community. Our children
always go when we go."

Again the evangelist studied the woman. "Sister,"

he said, "will you listen to a plain word without being offended?"

"Yes, sir, you can tell me anything you wish, and I shall not feel hurt. Give me your very best advice, no matter what it may be."

"Madam, your children are not being saved because your eyes are dry." The preacher turned away, and the mother went home.

She wept and and prayed all night long. The next morning she gave her husband his breakfast and waited for the children to get up. When they were all about the breakfast table, the mother turned to her older boy. "Johnnie, I've been praying as hard as I could that you might give your soul to Christ. Johnnie, will you take Christ as your Savior?"

The younger boy, named Edwin, hastily stood up, pushed back his chair, dropped his napkin on the table, and ran out of the room. The mother paid no attention to him, but kept on pleading with the first son. The Lord had mellowed the boy's heart. After some minutes, the mother and son knelt by the side of the dining-room table, and the mother had the infinite joy of praying her son into the kingdom of God. Right then and there he accepted Christ.

Late that afternoon, while the mother was in the kitchen working over the evening meal, Edwin came in to throw himself on his mother's neck. "Mother," he cried, "I'm saved! I've been saved! I've accepted Christ as my Savior! I am going forward tonight! Is Johnnie? Is Johnnie?"

"Yes, darling, Johnnie has given his heart to Jesus; but tell me, where have you been? What has happened to you?"

"Mamma, last night I could not sleep. I got up out

of bed, started downstairs to go to the icebox to get
something to eat, and some milk. I passed your door.
I thought I heard you crying. I tiptoed in. You were
stretched out on the floor praying, asking God to save
Johnnie and me. I didn't go into the kitchen. I went
back upstairs and cried myself to sleep. This morning
when you started talking to Johnnie, I just could not
stand any more. I ran out to the cotton patch, and I've
been there praying ever since. I have trusted Christ. I
know Jesus has saved me."

That night that mother had the infinite joy of leading
her two precious sons to the altar of God, to Christ and
into the church. Beloved, I have been in all sorts of
revivals, in churches, in brush arbors, in tents, in taber-
nacles, in school auditoriums, in theaters, in cotton
sheds. I have seen landslides for Christ. I have had
my heart broken many times over the paucity of results.
After these few years of humble yet many experiences
in preaching, I can sincerely, spiritually say I have
never seen a revival of any size, of any great propor-
tions, that was not paid for by the tears and the agony
of some of God's people. We shall never win these
great victories some of our hearts are longing for dry-
eyed. Gethsemane and Calvary must always precede
Pentecost. We need travailing Christians.

There is plenty of cause for travail, for passion, for
compassion, for tears. Think of the numberless hosts
of our fellow church-members who have lost the joy of
their salvation, who have become cold and indifferent
to the things of God and of His Christ. Think of the
literal thousands on our church rolls who never darken
the doors of their churches, who never pray a prayer,
give a penny, or make any sort of an effort to win the
lost to Christ. Think of the conduct of many of those

who do come to church on Sundays, only to serve the world and the flesh the rest of the week. Think of the hosts of our office-bearers—men, women, young people, filling responsible positions in our organized activities, whose lives are cluttered up with the things of this world, barren, powerless, fruitless. Think of the great numbers of churches of every denomination and persuasion who report no or heart-breakingly few converts and baptisms.

Turn away from our churches now. Let your minds dwell on the moral conditions of our nation—on the gambling, drinking, adultery, divorce, Sabbath-breaking, filthy literature. What an ocean of iniquity has swept across our land! How the devil has enthroned himself in every sphere of activity, in the high places and in the low! Consider the multitudes of unsaved men, women, children engaged in the *dans macabre* of sin, the devil drumming the tempo as their feet beat on the maddening descent into hell. Increasing in numbers with every passing day, the churches, Sunday-schools, revivals, missions, lagging fearfully behind, these multiplied myriads of immortal souls are plunging deeper and deeper into sin and indifference, getting ruder, coarser, harder, more unconcerned. Billy Sunday said that it was harder to win a fifteen-year-old boy for Christ at the end of his ministry than it was to win a seventy-year-old man when he first began to preach Christ.

Meditate upon these facts. Let them burn into your minds, throb in your hearts, ache in your souls. They will drive you to your knees in an agony of passionate travail that will make you over in your concern for and conduct toward your fellow-man. You can see very readily that ordinary, every-day lackadaisical methods lacking fire, empty of passion, lukewarm in intensity, will retire defeated before the marshalled hosts of Satan. No! We need passion, travail, weeping! It was only by the hot-hearted pressure of Elisha's body that the Shunnamite's son was brought back unto life. It will take the burning-hearted, the sacrificially-surrendered prayers and toil of the people of God to arouse into life this generation so palpably dead in trespasses and sins.

"But," you will say to me, "tell us, preacher, what does it mean to travail? What are the implications in the words of the mighty prophet?" Beloved, three things are involved in Isaiah's plea, in Isaiah's challenge, in Isaiah's cry.

First, there must be the travail of *separation*. There can be no power without surrender. Before a corn of wheat can produce grain, it must die. Before Jesus could become the Savior of a lost world, He had to perish on Calvary's cross. Before Moses could become the commander-in-chief of the Lord's people, he had to die the forty years in Midian's back lands. Before Saul could become Paul, he had to go through a Gethsemane, a Calvary experience, to himself, to his people, to his office, to his preconceived notions. That is the rule of eternity! That is the dictum of God! No death, no life! No price, no power! "Come ye out from among them and be ye separate," is still the clarion call of the Holy Spirit. They must "be clean that bear the vessels of the Lord," is still the *sine qua non* requirement in the service of the Redeemer. It will cost travail to divorce oneself from the world, to give up pleasures, some of them seemingly legitimate, to forsake friends, to turn your back upon loved ones, even though you have to tear chunks of your hearts out to do it. Separation comes high, but it leads to God-promised victory, success, fruitfulness. Where do you stand? Search your heart. Nay, better, permit the Holy Spirit to do it. Turn over every key to every room in your being. Hold nothing back, Ananiases and Sapphiras are still too common among us. Follow Him as He points out every secret sin, every evil thought, every unholy ambition, every worldly reservation. As He directs you, by the agony that loved you, by the cross that bought you, by the blood that washed you, give up, give up anything, everything, all things that are in any way disturbing, dishonoring, disgracing. Do not fear. Do not hesitate. God wants nothing from you selfishly. It is all for your own good, for your own happiness, for your own usefulness. Turn yourself over unreservedly into the hands of the Master. Yes, He may take you, may break you, may torment you, may mould you into the white heat of His love and power. But, oh, when He is through with you, when He gives you back to yourself that you may serve Him unconstrainedly in the beauty of holiness and virtue of love, you will be a polished instrument fit for the hands of the Great Mechanic. Yes, there must be the travail of separation. God is not looking for golden vessels, but for clean ones, for empty ones.

Second, there must be the travail of *intercession.* Prayer is power. Much prayer is much power. Little prayer is little power. No prayer is no power. There is no substitute for intercession, no short-cut into it. Earthly power is costly. Heavenly power is beyond computation, valuable. The price of it is absolute separation and unending intercession. May I be permitted to include every form of prayer in that one word, *intercession.* Study the experiences of the ages. Delve

into the lives, the writings, the works, the victories of
the mighty souls of every generation. Power followed
prayer. Souls were won, churches built, missionaries
sent out, money raised, Satan overcome, in the persistent intensity of passionate prayer. The secret of
the success of the apostles, of the first-century Christians, of the Augustines, of the Luthers, of the Knoxes,
of the Husses, of the Wesleys, of the Whitefields, of the
Moodys, of the numberless others who wrought righteousness in the power of the Lord, always has been
separation and supplication. It is the same today. O
dear God, if only our preachers, if only our office-
bearers, if only our teachers, if only our fathers, our
mothers, our church-members, would realize the way
of power, would take the steps of separation and supplication, what a mighty revival would sweep our land!
How our lives, our homes, our schools, our businesses,
our governments, our national and international en-
tanglements and embarrassments, would be changed!
Lord, pour out upon us, even as Thou hast promised,
the Spirit of grace and supplication.

This intercession must cover the earth. There must
be prayer for ourselves, that our own hearts may be
made right, our own lives stretched out on the altar,
our own souls filled and thrilled with the Holy Spirit.
Pray that we ourselves may be used of God to fish for
men. Pray that our own testimony may be conqueringly
constraining.

There must be prayer for each other, prayer that
will bear up our preachers, our deacons, stewards,
elders, teachers, officers, to the throne of grace, to melt
their hearts, to move their souls, to empower them for
service. Prayer will do more and go farther toward
strengthening, encouraging, enlightening, inspiring these

whom God has placed in responsible positions than anything else we or they can do. There must be burning, incessant, intercessory prayer for those of our fellow-Christians, church-members, who have wandered away from Christ, drifted out into sin. Prayer will constrain them to come back into God's service.

There must be prayer for the unsaved. Oh, how they need our prayers! They are lost in their sins, on the road to eternal destruction. Their souls are forfeited to Satan. They have no strength, no spiritual wisdom of their own, no inclination toward God. They will not pray for themselves. We who love them, who yearn for their salvation, who know the Savior, must pray them into the kingdom. There is no hope for them otherwise. They will drift on and on, growing colder, harder, deeper in sin, more indifferent with every passing day. Oh, let our prayers rise up for them in a fountain of travail. Let us immerse them in a sea of prayer. Let us give God no rest until His mercy is extended to these precious souls.

Third, there must be the travail of *visitation*, of personal soul-winning. That is the climax, the very capstone of all our travailing. With lives separated unto the Lord, with hearts, souls, minds, knees, bowed before God in the ecstasy of intercession, we receive the commission of the Lord to go afield and reap a harvest for Jesus. That is one of the chief secrets of the success of the early Christians. There was very little if any of the distinction between preacher and people. All were preachers, gospelers, evangelists, duty-bound, soul-obligated, God-sent, Spirit-empowered to witness and to win the lost. Wherever they went, whatever they did, regardless of circumstances and conditions, the primary purpose, the foremost thought, the

chiefest passion of their hearts was the salvation of
the souls of men. We shall never have great revivals,
we shall never have truly great, spiritual, Scriptural
churches until our people go back to the sense of
personal, apostolic, first-century responsibility.

We must all go. We must all do religious visitation.
We must all reap the harvest. That is doing the work
of the Master. That is literally following in the footsteps of the Lord. That is carrying out the Great Commission. We preachers must lead the parade. You
deacons, church officers, Sunday-school teachers, leaders
of our people, fathers, mothers, sons, daughters, all of
you, every one of you, as an army with conquering
banners must share the burden and brunt of this great
battle. God will use us to answer our prayers, to overcome Satan, to glorify the Master, to sweep in souls.

It is difficult work, sometimes tiring, disappointing,
disheartening, discouraging. Some rebuff us. Some
abuse us. Some are so coldly, bitterly, cruelly indifferent they tear our hearts. Some promise and break
their promises. Some come out for the Lord and then
drift back into sin. The devil seems to anticipate every
move we make, throws every sort of an obstacle in our
way, introduces every kind of a difficulty. It is trying,
testing, troubling toil. But, oh, thank God for some of
the victories we win. What greater joy can come to
the mortal soul than to help in the salvation of some
poor sinner! What reward can this world offer that is
even within seeing distance of the thrill of receiving the
gratitude of some man, woman, child that you have
prayed through and plead through into the kingdom of
the Lord! Think of the joy as it will increase with
the passing of the years, as the influences you have
started in the lives of wept-in souls spread out and out

in greater and ever increasing circles. Think of the value of the reward, the crown that shines brighter than the sun, moon, and stars, the crown of the soul-winner.

Just permit me to close with an illustration from my own poor ministry. During the first year of my ministry, I held a revival in a very tiny village in Oklahoma. The Lord blessed the campaign. One afternoon the pastor and this preacher were walking down the highway, knocking on doors, inviting people to Christ and the church. We came to a farm-yard. This preacher started to open the gate. "It's no use going in there," said the pastor, stopping him; "there lives in this house a family of five—a father, mother, three children. None of them are Christians. The woman is the most wicked character in this town. She is a common harlot. She won't come to church anyway."

"Let's try her, anyway," answered this preacher, opening the gate and walking up on the porch, with the pastor following. He knocked on the door. The woman opened it and stood in the narrow opening, looking at the two men before her.

"Lady, my name is Appelman. I am the evangelist. This is Brother B., pastor of the Baptist church in this town. We have come to invite you to our revival. Our services are at eight o'clock every night. Will you come tonight?"

"I don't go to church, thank you."

"But, lady, one time will not hurt you. Do come tonight."

"If I come to church, the building will cave in."

"No it won't. We are holding the services in the open air."

After some more pleading and persuasion, the woman promised to come the next night. She came a little late.

The usher led her all the way down to the front to
place her on one of the very front pews. Two women,
who had been sitting there, got up and walked back
into the crowd. The preacher began to understand a
bit better the reason for the woman's condition. When
the service was over, the preacher hurried to the woman.

"Sister, if there is anything I can do or these people
can do to make up to you for what happened tonight,
tell me, and I shall see that it is done."

"Never mind, I am used to being treated in just that
way. I'm coming back tomorrow night. I liked your
sermon and appreciate your interest."

The next night she came back. The song service
seemed to move her, the sermon to melt her. When the
invitation was given, she was the very first to come to
the altar to kneel in prayer. Others came. The pastor
and the evangelist knelt down by the mourner's side,
and after some prayer and Scripture quoting, she sur-
rendered her heart to Christ and offered herself for
membership in one of the churches of the town. Her
husband came in as well as the first of her children.

Three years later, this preacher, then a student in
the seminary in Fort Worth, held a meeting in the
larger town ten miles north of the village where the
woman still lived. At the end of the two weeks, early
on a Monday morning, he was hurrying back to school,
to wife, to Texas. The road led past the home of the
woman. She was out in the yard hanging out washing.
The preacher saluted her with the car horn. She
waved him down, made him stop, and came out to the
automobile.

"Brother preacher, please come out and have breakfast with us. Doc [that was her husband] has just
taken the cows out. He'll be right back."

"Sorry, sister, but I cannot stop. I've been away from home and school for two weeks. I am behind in my work. I have a hundred and ninety miles to drive yet. I just must go on. You will have to excuse me."

The woman put her hands into the car, placed them on the hands of the preacher, on the steering wheel, and with tears streaming down her face, said, "Brother Preacher, we love you, all of us. As long as there is a W—— home in the world, we'll never forget what you have done for us."

The preacher said, "Thank God, not me, sister. I am not entitled to it. The Lord has saved your soul."

He started the car and drove off. Coming to a little bend in the road out of sight of the woman, the preacher stopped his car in the grass off the pavement. He took out his handkerchief, spread it on the steering wheel, and made an altar there. Lifting his face to the heavens, with his heart's blood and soul's affection punctuating every word he spoke, he said: "Lord Jesus, it cost me father, mother, brothers, sister, kinsfolk, friends, money, property, law office, everything almost a man holds dear in life, to become a Christian, to surrender to preach the gospel. Lord, if you never give me another thing as long as I live, you have already paid me in full."

The preacher meant it then, He means it now. Every time the Holy Spirit uses him to bring a precious soul to the feet of Jesus, his cup of joy, of blessing, of compensation, of reward runs over. God, give us, each of us, all of us, the grace to travail for souls until Zion brings forth her children. In Jesus' name. Amen.

IX

I KNOW THERE IS A HEAVEN

After this I beheld, and, lo, a great multitude, which no man could number, of all nations, and kindreds, and people, and tongues, stood before the throne, and before the Lamb, clothed with white robes, and palms in their hands; and cried with a loud voice, saying, Salvation to our God which sitteth upon the throne, and unto the Lamb. And all the angels stood round about the throne, and about the elders and the four beasts, and fell before the throne on their faces, and worshipped God, saying, Amen: Blessing, and glory, and wisdom, and thanksgiving, and honour, and power, and might, be unto our God for ever and ever. Amen. And one of the elders answered, saying unto me, What are these which are arrayed in white robes? and whence came they? And I said unto him, Sir, thou knowest. And he said unto me, These are they which came out of great tribulation, and have washed their robes, and made them white in the blood of the Lamb. Therefore are they before the throne of God, and serve him day and night in his temple: and he that sitteth on the throne shall dwell among them. They shall hunger no more, neither thirst any more; neither shall the sun light on them, nor any heat. For the Lamb which is in the midst of the throne shall feed them, and shall lead them unto living fountains of waters: and God shall wipe away all tears from their eyes.

—Rev. 7: 9-17

And I saw a new heaven and a new earth: for the first heaven and the first earth were passed away; and there was no more sea. And I John saw the holy city, new Jerusalem, coming down from God out of heaven, prepared as a bride adorned for her husband. And I heard a great voice out of heaven saying, Behold, the tabernacle of God is with men, and he will dwell with them, and they shall be his people, and God himself shall be with them, and be their God. And God shall wipe away all tears from their eyes; and there shall be no more death, neither sorrow, nor crying, neither shall there be any more pain: for the former things are passed away.—REV. 21: 1-4

And I saw no temple therein: for the Lord God Almighty and the Lamb are the temple of it. And the city had no need of any sun, neither of the moon, to shine in it: for the glory of God did lighten it, and the Lamb is the light thereof. And the nations of them which are saved shall walk in the light of it: and the kings of the earth do bring their glory and honour into it. And the gates of it shall not be shut at all by day: for there shall be no night there. And they shall bring the glory and honour of the nations into it. And there shall in no wise enter into it anything that defileth, neither whatsoever worketh abomination, or maketh a lie: but they which are written in the Lamb's book of life.—REV. 21: 22-27

HEAVEN is a prepared place for a prepared people. It is one of the mightiest, if not the very mightiest, rewards God Almighty holds out to those who accept His Son as Savior and by persistent well-doing show forth their title to eternal fellowship with the hosts of glory. It is a joyous, noble, inspiring, cheering doctrine. It has encouraged the martyr at the stake and sustained the bed-ridden Christian tormented by the burden, the weight, the ailments of the flesh. Its message has charmed our childhood, heartened our maturity, inspired our old age. It has given us the brave fortitude to bear the trials and temptations of life with unbowed head and unfaltering step. There is not a soul among us, no matter how seemingly indifferent or unconcerned, who is not at times—and these times come oftener and oftener with the advance of the years—brought face to face with the problems of the reality, of the very existence of heaven. It is my purpose, God aiding, to bring to your minds, to your hearts, to your souls some of the glorious, victorious truths about heaven, its citizens, its perfections, its conditions, and, perhaps most of all, to point out to you what you must do to get there; then to plead with you in all the passion of my soul that you put your feet by faith in the way of the cross that leads to God and to heaven. My outline is simple, brief, and, I hope, to the point. I know there is a heaven. I know what kind of a place it is. I know I am going there. I beseech you to come with me.

I. I KNOW THERE IS A HEAVEN

Fairness says so. Decency, justice, rightness, honor, honesty, common sense, demand it. Where would be the justice, the boasted equity of God, were there no heaven? Christians do not always have the best of it in this life. Many of them are poor. Many of them are sick. Many of them are oppressed, afflicted, tormented. There is very little reward for them in this life. The gods of this world press upon them and beset them on every hand. Throughout the generations, they have had to pay the price, sometimes with their lives, for the testimony of their love and loyalty to the Son of God and to His church and cause. Where is there a continent, a clime, a country where Christians have not known the frowns and the persecutions of the children of the world? Imprisoned, whipped, outlawed, ostracized, crucified, staked, beheaded, torn asunder, thrown to the wild beasts, made sport of by the cruel bloodthirstiness of the maddened maniac mobs, where in this life, where in this world, have the servants of the Lord been rewarded for their zeal, for their constancy, for their sacrifices? Pray, tell me, what honors came in

this life to beheaded Paul, to crucified Peter, to flayed
Bartholomew, to slain James? Show me, if you can,
the gold and valuable raiment, the houses and lands,
the plaudits and pleasures that fell to the lot of John
Bunyan either before or after the twelve bitter years
in Bedford jail. Then look about you. See how loyal,
loving Christians have to and do deny themselves the
pleasures, sometimes even the very necessities of this
life, to make themselves more effective, more serviceable in the work of their Master. Then look elsewhere
in the milling throngs. Is it not a fact that the children
of darkness, the disobedient unbelievers, living in the
paths of sin, seem only too often to have the better
part of it on earth? Tell me, can it be possible that
this is the way it should be and always will be? Tell
me, can you believe that the sacrificial saint and the
selfish sinner will meet God and enjoy the same conditions in the life beyond? No! Fairness requires that
there be a difference. Heaven is the difference. Fairness says so.

Feeling says so. There is something in my heart as
there is surely in your hearts, some affection, some
emotion, some drawing, pulling, echoing something that
tells us again and again that there is a life beyond the
skies, a life with God, a life of joy, of tenderness,
purity, holiness, peace, where these troublesome, trying,
tempestuous burdens that afflict us will be sloughed off
and we shall stand free and upright in the sight of God
and of His Christ. Look into the very depths of your
souls. Tell me, is it not so? Is there not in your hearts
a longing for the fellowship of God, for the communion
of Christ, for the freedom of the Holy Spirit, for the
presence of the angels? That feeling was placed there
by God. It has grown with the passing of the years.

Surely God would not have endowed you with that
yearning, kept it alive all these years, unless He meant
to satisfy it in His own good time, in His own good
will. This life cannot be the all in all. Our feelings
prohibit such a thought. This earth cannot be the entire
course of our existence, with the cold grave as the end
of it. The God-implanted, the Christ-authenticated, the
Holy-Spirit-evoked feelings of our souls cannot so deliberately, so desperately beguile us. No! There must
be a heaven. There is a heaven. Feeling says so.

Faith says so. Faith is confidence in the Word of
God. The Book unmistakably, definitely, shoutingly,
pressingly, imperatively teaches that there is a heaven.
Doubt it, and the whole Christian system is exploded,
the Bible is questioned, hope is blackened, faith is
blinded, and of all God's creatures, we are the most
miserable. But who doubts it? Some misguided, so-
called intelligent, half-baked pseudo-scientist, who in
the superlative "infinity" of his newly received book
information and laboratory technique, thinking himself
some Columbus-like discoverer of an America of scien-
tific exploration, refuses to credit anything that he
cannot squeeze into his geometric theorem or physical
test tube. But we know better, thank God! Those of
us who are willing to be enlightened by the Spirit of
God, even though the enlightenment and the information may go directly against the grain of preconceived
notions and opinions, have the singing, shouting, satisfactory assurance that Jesus spoke the fact of God when
He said, "In my Father's house are many mansions . . .
I go to prepare a place for you." Faith says so. Backed
up by, founded on the inerrant, unchangeable, unmistakable, eternal Word of God, regardless of gainsaying
scientist or philosopher or unbeliever. Faith clarions to

the world that Christians are seeking a city whose founder and builder is God, a city of peace, of rest, of bliss, of reward. There is a heaven. Faith says so.

II. I KNOW WHAT KIND OF A PLACE HEAVEN IS

My heart tells me. My soul whispers it to me. My mind loves to dwell upon it. But, best of all, most assuring of all, safest of all, most satisfactory of all, the Bible definitely describes it. It is good exercise, inspiring practice, uplifting meditation, to run the references in the old Book on Heaven.

It is a prepared place. It is not an accidental, fortuitous conglomeration of a jerry-built something. It is a prepared place. God is its architect. Christ is its superintendent. The Holy Spirit is its foreman of construction. The holy angels are its builders. It is a work of art, a labor of love. There is nothing accidental or incidental in it. Every inch of its mighty, magnificent construction is dictated by the compassionate heart and altogether wise head of the Father. With definite, minute consideration for the welfare of the saints, for their tastes and distastes, for their likes and dislikes, the angels are leaving nothing out that will add to our peace, to our happiness, to our singing joy. It is in every detail a thing of beauty, a joy forever. Its climate is salubrious. Its grasses, trees, flowers, are of breath-taking beauty. Its streets are paved with gold. Its buildings are of the costliest, everlasting marble. Its government is in the hands of the Prince of peace. The Holy Spirit is its superintendent of education. The angels make up its teaching staffs. There are no jailhouses, no prisons, no reformatories, no hospitals, no orphanages, no old folks' homes, no drugstores, no doctors, no dentists, no lawyers, no courts, no blind, no deaf, no dumb, no cripples, no weak, no aged, no feeble. Sin and Satan are banished forever. Nothing that is unclean or defileth in any way will be permitted to enter through its wide gates. There is nothing on earth to which we can compare it. The human mind cannot comprehend nor can the human tongue describe the glories of that eternal, prepared place.

It is a populated place. John says he saw a great multitude which no man could number of every nation, kindred, and tribe, out of all the earth. Thank God for that. From every continent, clime, country, color, creed over all the earth, Jew and Gentile, black and white, Catholic, Protestant, Baptist, young and old, rich and poor, weak and strong, educated, ignorant, they have all been bidden to the marriage supper of the Lamb, and myriads have accepted the invitation. What a crowd that will be! What a place of meeting, of greeting, of rejoicing that will be! Many of you have fathers, mothers, brothers, sisters, husbands, wives, sons, daughters, that have crossed chilly Jordan before you. Thanks be unto God, you will all clasp hands and rejoice in the presence of God nevermore to endure the pangs, the bitter pangs of parting. All of us have friends that were as dear to us as our own flesh and blood whom God has called up higher. They, too, are waiting for us, waiting to welcome us into that fellowship of eternal bliss. Yes, heaven is a peopled place, filled with those who have washed their garments and made them white in the blood of the Lamb.

It is a perfect place. The wisdom, the grace, the power of God assure and insure its perfections. There can be no flaws there, no mistakes, no something to have been left out or something to have been put in.

There are no disappointments in heaven, no discourage-
ments, no disheartenings. There is no sorrow in glory,
no suffering, no pain. There are no tears in the presence
of God, and the sable-hued angel of death walks not
its golden streets. None of the toil, none of the trial,
none of the tribulation of earth find a resting-place
there. The waters of the river of life flow abundantly
to be freely quaffed by all unto the renewal of youth,
vigor, vitality. We never grow old up there, but in the
very prime of virile manhood and clean womanhood
serve the Lord forever. Its joys flow on eternally. Its
bliss knows no end. Its sweets never cloy, so varied are
they and attractive. It is small wonder that those who
have seen the vision of it by faith are longingly homesick for that land of endless day. Men have dreamed
of Utopias, have envisioned the perfections of an earthly
state, only to fall back in defeated dismay because flesh
and blood could not achieve the banishment of the dis-
pleasing, the disturbing, the disheartening, the disappointing. It is only in the glory land that these beauties,
that these joys, that these lofty dreams will find fruition.
There and there only will the fatherhood of God and
the brotherhood of man come to an endless realization.

III. I Know I Am Going There

I have the assurance of that fact. It shouts in my
heart, sings in my soul, sounds in my mind. I know
beyond peradventure, beyond question, beyond doubt,
beyond any sort of uncertainty that I am bound for
the Promised Land, that one day I shall tread its golden
streets, that one day I shall hear the angels sing, that
one day I shall meet all of my precious friends who
have gone on before me, that one day I shall see my
blessed Savior face to face.

I know I am going there because I am saved. My

entrance into the glory land is not postulated upon the facts that I am a circumcised Jew, a regenerated Christian, a Baptist, a preacher of the gospel, an evangelist, that, to the glory of God, the Holy Spirit has used my prayers, my tears, my testimony to win souls for Christ. No, I am going there because I am saved, because I have believed on the Lord Jesus Christ, because I have confessed Him before men, because my sins are forgiven, because my name is written in the Lamb's Book of life. I am basing my hope, nay, my assurance of salvation on the unchangeable, unshakeable, unmistakable Word of God. God has told me: "For God so loved the world that he gave his only begotten son that whosoever believeth in him should not perish but have everlasting life." Jesus said, "Whosoever confesseth me before men, him will I also confess before my Father which is in heaven." "I am the resurrection and the life: he that believeth on me, though he were dead, yet shall he live: and he that liveth and believeth on me shall never die." Paul said, "If thou shalt confess with thy mouth the Lord Jesus, and shalt believe in thine heart that God has raised him from the dead, thou shalt be saved." I have done all that. I have put my utter faith in the Lord Jesus Christ. I have believed on Him. I have confessed Him before men. By His own unalterable, Holy Word, I know I am saved. I am going to heaven.

I know I am going there because I am sealed, sealed in the eternal love, in the eternal purpose, in the eternal power, by the eternal Spirit of God. The matchless promises of God's Word tell me so. Hear the glorious truths of the Book of Ephesians: "Blessed be the God and Father of our Lord Jesus Christ, who hath blessed us with all spiritual blessings in heavenly places

in Christ: according as he hath chosen us in him before
the foundation of the world, that . . . . having predes-
tinated us unto the adoption of children by Jesus Christ
. . . . wherein he hath made us accepted in the beloved . . . . that in the dispensation of the fulness of
times he might gather together in one all things in
Christ . . . . in whom also we have obtained an inheritance . . . . who first trusted in Christ . . . . in whom ye
also trusted, after that ye heard the word of truth, the
gospel of your salvation: in whom also after that ye
believed, ye were sealed with that Holy Spirit of
promise, which is the earnest of our inheritance until
the redemption of his purchased possession, unto the
praise of his glory." Need I add anything to that mar-
velous doxology? Surely not. Surely the Word of God
needs no commendation, needs no bolstering up from
any poor earthling such as I am. I know I am going
to heaven because when I accepted Christ Jesus as my
Savior my eternal destiny was sealed in the covenant of
God's grace, signed and sealed by the blood of the Lord
Jesus Christ.

I know I am going to heaven because I am sustained.
All along the journey from earth to heaven, since the
day I first accepted the Christ as my Redeemer, God
has made ample, abundant, satisfactory provision for
my welfare. There is nothing I need, material, mental,
physical, spiritual, that is not abundantly available to
me according to the riches of God's grace by and in
Christ Jesus. I have the gift of the Holy Spirit to encourage and empower me. I have the promises of the
blessed Word to cash on the bank of heaven for all
my needs. I have proved again and again that Matt.
6: 33, "Seek ye first the kingdom of God and his
righteousness, and all these things will be added unto

you," is the absolute word of the most honorable Gentleman in time and eternity. I know from personal, definite, dependable experience that He "is able to keep me from falling and to present me faultless before the presence of his glory with exceeding joy." I can shout with all the fervor of my soul, the words of Peter, "Blessed be the God and Father of our Lord Jesus Christ, which according to his abundant mercy hath begotten us again unto a lively hope by the resurrection of Jesus Christ from the dead, to an inheritance incorruptible, and undefiled, and that fadeth not away, reserved in heaven for you [for us], who are kept by the power of God through faith unto salvation ready to be revealed in the last day." Yes, I know I am going to heaven because I am kept by the power of God, sustained by the grace of God, supported by the Spirit of God, as I journey from earth to heaven.

IV. I Beseech You to Come with Me

Now permit me a last word. As God gave me utterance, I have told you why I know there is a heaven; what kind of a place it is; why I know I am going there. May I passionately, earnestly, urgently, *beseech you to go with me to heaven.* You may if you will. It is altogether dependent upon your willingness. There is but one thing in your way: not your sins; Christ can and will wash those away; not your weaknesses, the Holy Spirit can conquer those in you. There is nothing in your way but your own, "I will." This hour, if you are ready to say to God, "Lord have mercy on me, a sinner," God stands ready to enroll you in the citizenship of heaven.

God wants you to be saved. He says so. "As I live, saith the Lord God, I have no joy in the death of the wicked, but that the wicked might turn from his wicked way. Turn ye! Turn ye! For why will ye die?" Paul says so. "For this is good and acceptable in the sight of God and our Saviour, who will have all men to be saved and to come to the knowledge of the truth." Peter says so. "God is not slack concerning his promises as men count slackness, but is longsuffering to usward, not willing that any should perish, but that all should come to repentance." Yes, God Almighty wants you to Himself, with Himself, for Himself, in heaven. He says so.

Christ died to pave a way for you into heaven. He suffered, bled, died under the burden and weight of your sins that sinless, spotless, stainless, you may tread the courts of glory. "He hath made him to be sin for us, who knew no sin, that we might be made the righteousness of God in him." "Christ hath redeemed us from the curse of the law, being made a curse for us." "But now once in the end of the world hath he appeared to put away sin by the sacrifice of himself . . . . and unto them that look for him shall he appear the second time without sin unto salvation." "Unto him that loved us, and washed us from our sins in his own blood, and hath made us kings and priests unto God and his Father; to him be glory and dominion forever and ever. Amen." The blood of the cross will make you fit, favorable, acceptable at the throne of grace. John, in describing the multitudes in heaven that no man could number, said of them, "These are they which came out of great tribulation, and have washed their robes, and made them white in the blood of the Lamb." This blood cleansing is for all the saints, for all the faithful, for all the believing, for you.

The Holy Spirit invites you to the marriage supper of the Lamb. Even before the coming of Christ, the invitation was issued to all of the children of men: "Ho, everyone that thirsteth, come ye to the waters, and he that hath no money: come ye, buy and eat; yea, come, buy wine and milk without money and without price." In the Parable of the Marriage Supper of the King's Son, to which many were invited, the Lord Jesus definitely teaches the broadness, the wideness, the inclusiveness of the invitation to salvation and heaven. The very Bible itself closes in Rev. 22:17 with the mighty, world-wide invitation of the Spirit and the church to enter the mansions of rest, "And the Spirit and the bride say, Come. And let him that heareth say, Come. And let him that is athirst come. And whosoever will, let him take of the water of life freely." There can be no misunderstanding of an appeal like that.

Tonight, brother, sister, the gates of glory swing wide open for your entrance. God is bending down from the throne. Jesus is reaching out His pierced hands to you. The Holy Spirit is softly whispering the gentle welcome of the invitation. Will you accept it? Some years ago, one of the engineers of the Chicago, Milwaukee, and St. Paul Railroad, a superb Christian man, built his home by the side of the right of way. He had a six-year-old daughter. Every day the engineer, in passing his home, pulled the cord of the engine's whistle to greet his loved ones. The little daughter got into the habit of climbing on the fence to wave at her daddy as he passed. One day she overbalanced herself and tumbled into the ravine at the foot of the tracks. Her father came home that night to find her in bed with a bruised, scratched body. "Darling," he said to her, "you must not climb that fence anymore. The next time you might hurt yourself pretty badly."

"But, Daddy," replied the child, "I want to see you

and wave at you when you go past. How will I do it
if I cannot climb up on the fence?"

"I'll tell you what I'll do," answered the father;
"tomorrow before I leave I'll take a board out of the
fence. This evening and every other evening when I
go past, you can stick your head and shoulders through
that hole and see me and wave at me."

The man did just as he said. From then on, daily,
when the train sped past, the whistle blowing, the child
pressed herself into the fence and waved hand and
handkerchief to the much loved father. The days sped
past. The winter came. The little girl contracted a
severe cold that rapidly developed into double pneumonia. The man took time out of his job and sat night
and day by the bed of his darling. The doctors did
the best they could, but God wanted that flower in His
own garden. The girl grew steadily worse until one
day the family physician came out to call the father
into the sickroom with the dreadful news that the child
was dying. The father and mother stood at the foot of
the bed watching their precious baby. Pale of face,
eyes closed, she lay there on her back in her little bed.
Minutes went past. After a time, she opened her eyes.
Noticing the tears of her parents, she whispered in a
faint little voice, "Daddy, Mamma, why are you
crying?"

The father and mother, choked with their emotions,
were unable to answer. They looked at the good doctor.
The doctor turned to the child and, taking her small
hand in his, gently told her that her father and mother
were weeping because she was leaving them to be with
Jesus. Again the child looked up into the face of her
father. "Daddy," she said, "you mean I am going to
die?" The father dropped to his knees by the side of

the bed and pressed his face against the face of his loved child. "Yes, darling," he whispered, "you are leaving Daddy and Mamma to go to be with Jesus." The girl whimpered a little in soft crying. Then she bethought herself of something and began to comfort the mourning ones. "Daddy," she said, "Mamma, don't cry. When I get to heaven, the first thing I am going to do is tell Jesus about you. I am going to tell Him what a good Daddy and Mamma you were and how you always talked to me about Him. Then I am going to ask Jesus to take a board out of the wall around heaven. Every day I shall go to that opening and watch for you. When I see you coming, I shall wave at you to show you where I am that you may come to me."

Brethren and sisters, that is just what Jesus is doing for us and to us right now. Bending over the battlements of glory, His pierced hands stretched out to us, He is beckoning us to come to Him. He is longingly, yearningly, pleadingly, anxiously waiting for you. Will you this very moment accept His invitation? Will you, in humble, penitent, childlike, yet bold, trusting faith, come to the blessed Savior right now, that you, together with the great multitude of us, may start on the journey to the Promised Land, never to finish until you stand complete in the Lord Jesus Christ before the throne of God in the glorious heavens? God, give you the grace to come. For Jesus' sake. Amen.

Printed in the United States of America

CPSIA information can be obtained
at www.ICGtesting.com
Printed in the USA
BVHW031158130819
555687BV00002B/148/P

9 781432 594282